Spirits
Between the Bays
Series

Volume IV

In The
Vestibule

True ghost stories from
the Delmarva Peninsula
to the Jersey Shore

Ed Okonowicz

Myst and Lace Publishers, Inc.

Spirits Between the Bays
Volume IV
In the Vestibule
First Edition

ISBN 0-9643244-6-6

Published by
Myst and Lace Publishers, Inc.
1386 Fair Hill Lane
Elkton, Maryland 21921

Printed in the U.S.A.
by Modern Press

Artwork, Typography and Design
by Kathleen Okonowicz

Dedications

To Marie, my loving cousin, who has been so supportive
To Aunt Marie, for all her kindness.
And to my Uncle Paul, who reads these books too quickly.
Ed Okonowicz

To Gayle Remenick, my lifelong best friend.
We share a lifetime of dreams and memories.
Kathleen Burgoon Okonowicz

Acknowledgments

The author and illustrator appreciate the assistance of those
who have played an important role in this project.

Special thanks are extended to

Geraldine McKeown and
Sandy Longenecker
for their creative assistance;

and to

John Brennan,
Sue Moncure,
Ted Stegura and
Monica Witkowski
for their proofreading and suggestions;

and, of course,

particular appreciation to the ghosts and their hosts.

Also available from
Myst and Lace Publishers, Inc.

S̸pirits Between the Bays Series

Volume I
Pulling Back the Curtain
(October, 1994)

Volume II
Opening the Door
(March, 1995)

Volume III
Welcome Inn
(September, 1995)

Volume IV
In the Vestibule
(August, 1996)

Volume V
Presence in the Parlor
(Spring, 1997)

Stairway over the Brandywine
A Love Story
(February, 1995)

Possessed Possessions
Haunted Antiques, Furniture and Collectibles
(March, 1996)

Table of Contents

Legend and Lore

✣*The individuals involved have agreed to allow real names and actual locations to be used in this presentation of their story.*

Introduction

W e started by **Pulling Back the Curtain, Opening the Door** and encouraging you further with a **Welcome Inn.** And now, by your own choice, you've dared to enter the foyer of our most intriguing home.

In the Vestibule places you ever deeper into the *Spirits Between the Bays* series of true ghost tales. As in the first three volumes, this book includes eerie reports of ghostly sightings in hamlets, villages and cities in the 14 counties located in the three states between the Chesapeake and Delaware Bays.

In addition, we have responded to those readers who have provided a number of fascinating true tales that have taken place at unsettled sites slightly Beyond the Bays. Residents of Baltimore and Harford County, on Maryland's Western Shore, as well as visitors to the interior and coastal towns of New Jersey have shared excellent tales of unusually delightful horror and mystery. Since these fascinating stories were too good to pass up, we've expanded, ever so slightly, our geographical boundaries to offer a few true tales of terror that occurred in these neighboring areas.

Based on the popularity of **Welcome Inn,** Vol. III of our *Spirits Between the Bays* series, we have included a new public site—the Rose & Crown Pub & Restaurant in Lewes, Delaware—that readers will be able to visit.

At least one ghostly story that has occurred at an inn, restaurant or museum will be featured in every upcoming Spirits series volume, and it will be indicated with the bat symbol. This will give readers *who dare* new public sites to explore during their ghostly travels throughout the region.

Regular readers will notice that, in addition to stretching our geographical boundaries, **In the Vestibule** features a trio of stories focusing on reports of a mid-Atlantic version of *Bigfoot.* The accounts by these eyewitnesses should make one wonder if the monster of

1

the American Northwest might have a cousin roaming at night, nearby, through the fields and forests of the East and South.

Or, just maybe, these sightings are of the elusive spirits of primeval creatures who once roamed the area at will. Perhaps they return, in another form, from another dimension, during darkness to travel familiar paths they once followed during life.

You read . . . and you decide.

A pair of stories on haunted firehouses reinforces the fact that hauntings are not limited to decaying mansions and 200-year-old farmhouses. Ghosts can exist anywhere and are found just about everywhere.

"She was a regular ghost factory," said one faithful reader of our series, when discussing Patty Cannon, Delaware and Maryland's most famous murderess and 19th-century serial killer.

The story in this volume is based upon interviews with Delaware author Jerry Shields, who has written a book on Patty; George Figgs, one of her great-great-great-nephews; and Bob Wetherall, Dover library director, who currently is keeper of the murderess' skull.

Finally, we are pleased to feature our first guest author, Debby Lyons of Trappe, Maryland, who submitted an experience about the mysterious "Lady." Debby's well-written, true story is one we could not pass up, and we know our readers will enjoy her personal account of a series of unusual encounters with the unexplained.

We offer our sincere thanks to all those who shared the experiences featured in this volume, and those we are planning to include in future books in the series. We look forward to other unusual leads and personal stories that continue to arrive from our readers.

Until we meet again, in Vol. V: **Presence in the Parlor . . . .**

Happy Hauntings, and beware of black cats, broken mirrors and the hidden creatures that most certainly roam the dark corners of the night.

—Ed Okonowicz
in Fair Hill, Maryland,
at the northern edge of
the Delmarva Peninsula
—Fall 1996

Cousin Billy

L ola Hoffman currently lives in Delaware, but she will always remember growing up in Baltimore during the 1920s and '30s.

Her family's rowhouse was on West North Avenue, a major thoroughfare that was active with the excitement of passing trolleys and the distinctive, sing-song calls of street vendors.

Her father operated Ruxton's Pharmacy. Like other small businesses in those days, the family's living quarters were behind and above the store.

Sitting in the living room of her suburban, Newark home, Lola recalled the mysterious footsteps and unexplained noises that had occurred in that Baltimore home more than 50 years ago. Then, she added that her mother had the gift.

"My mother had ESP. She definitely did," said Lola, and she shared the following story as an example.

When Lola was in her late teens, her cousin, Billy, who was a few years older, moved into their Baltimore rowhouse.

"He was a sailor," Lola said. "He followed the water, so Billy didn't live with us year round. He would appear when his ship came into port and disappear just as suddenly when he was shipping out, on one of the oil tankers that he worked on.

"He was like a brother to me," Lola said. "We were really close. When he was in town, we'd go to the movies together, and he always brought me unusual gifts from the faraway places he visited."

Early one morning, while the chill was still in the air and a mist of dew coated the ship's metal railings, Billy was directing a loading on the docks. Suddenly, a loose piece of heavy pipe struck him in the head and he was taken to a hospital.

While he was recovering, Billy got word from one of his shipmates that his girlfriend in Louisiana had been shot. Apparently, Lola said, Billy took it pretty hard.

Spirits Between the Bays

When he was released from the hospital, Billy spent a short period at Lola's home and the family thought he had recovered from the ship accident and the bad news about his girlfriend's death.

"Usually, Billy would just take off when he was ready to go out with his next ship," Lola said. "And he had a habit of saying 'So long' as he walked down the hall, heading out toward the door.

"I remember, he had been in port for a few weeks by this time, and he was getting restless. We all could tell that he had to get back out to sea. One afternoon, my mother was entertaining a number of friends and Billy walked by, down the hallway. He just said, 'Good bye' and kept walking. Later, when we went in his room, we discovered that he hadn't taken his sea bag, and he never came back later to pick up his gear. We realized that he just wasn't right, that something was wrong, and we began to worry."

Soon afterwards, Lola's mother had a dream that Billy was at 1600 Light Street, located around the harbor. She repeated the address to her husband and Lola several times.

During those days, the Baltimore seaport was nothing like the modern, attractive, showcase-style Inner Harbor. It was a run down area lined with old warehouses, crumbling wharves, decrepit flop houses and dingy saloons. The area also was littered with a good number of wrecked and discarded boats, many in need of serious repair or disposal.

"My mother kept telling us that she dreamt Billy was at 1600 Light Street," Lola recalled, "but my father told her it was the harbor, and there was nothing there. Eventually, he agreed to take her down to show her that there was nothing at that address, so we all could be satisfied and put the issue to rest. When they found nothing, just a bunch of empty warehouses, Daddy called the police and reported Billy missing."

Soon they received a call that the police had found a young man floating in the water.

"His face was so swollen," Lola said, "that he didn't have any features and could hardly be identified. But Billy had a white streak that went straight down the center of his coal black hair. They used that to identify him."

Lola's father had a regular customer who worked as a captain on the city fire boat that patrolled the harbor.

"After Billy was found, the fire captain came into our store and said, 'I understand that it was your nephew that we picked up. We didn't realize it was a man, we thought it was a ship's buoy, floating out there.'

"My father asked, 'Where did you find him?'

"And the fire captain replied, 'At 1600 Light Street.'

"It was so uncanny," Lola said, "because he named 1600, not just Light Street, but the exact address. Of course, the area's gone now, because it's all the Inner Harbor there. My mother was very calm about it. All she said was, 'I knew he was there.' "

Apparently Billy had one more piece of unfinished business to complete before he ceased contact with the family and moved on.

Within a week of the funeral, Lola's mother experienced another dream. She saw Billy, in his bedroom, leaning against an overstuffed chair. Then he reached into his bureau, lifted up the paper that lined the bottom of one of the drawers, and pulled out a packet.

Holding the bundle of papers, in the dream, he said, "These are for you."

The next morning, Lola's mother went into the bedroom, looked in Billy's bureau drawer and discovered a number of bonds, with her name on them.

"Apparently, my mother had the 'gift,' " Lola said. "But that dream about Billy and the bonds, I think that was a little too much for her to handle. She didn't talk too much about it, but I could tell she always knew things, a lot more than she would let on."

The Phantom Firefighter

After attending dozens of ghost book signings at stores and in malls, I can usually tell when someone has an unusual experience to share. The person sort of stands and stares. But there's also a nervous type of hovering, caused by the struggle between a desire to keep moving and the feeling that both feet are cemented to the floor.

To break the awkward silence, I toss out the verbal bomb: "Do you have a ghost?" Almost immediately the person answers with a relief-filled "Yes!"

That's what happened at the Christiana Mall in Newark, Delaware, where I first met Chuck Knox, an ambulance driver for a South Jersey hospital. He hesitantly said he had experienced a series of ghostly events in a New Jersey firehouse.

My curiosity was sparked. We agreed to meet at a restaurant in Cape May, New Jersey, not far from his home, so I could hear his story.

It was a warm, fall afternoon. Most of the shops were open, and Chuck's wife, Linda, politely excused herself as soon as I arrived.

"She doesn't like to hear this kind of stuff," Chuck said, nodding in her direction as she exited the bar's antique, stained-glass door. "She's going to go shopping until we're done. She'll be back in about an hour."

I nodded. It's happened before. Sometimes it's the husband who leaves. This time it was the wife.

We had a corner booth to ourselves. Across the street we could see the rhythmic waves hitting the beach. It was fall, but it seemed more like spring outside.

Chuck looked younger than his 45 years, probably because of his trim physique and short, bristle brush haircut. His face was

6

thin and angular, but he had a youthful look when he flashed a quick, nervous, toothy smile.

The two pages of handwritten notes that he had prepared before my arrival were wrinkled by his tight grasp. He kept glancing at them. I got the impression that he was using the papers as a prop to avoid meeting my eyes while he shared his story.

If anyone was ever a living, breathing definition of nervous, it was Chuck Knox that Sunday at the beginning of our conversation.

"Before we start," Chuck said, his voice level slightly above a whisper, "you have to promise to change the names and the place this happened. I don't want to use the exact details. Members of the family are still in the town. I don't want to hurt them."

I nodded.

"I also want to say, for the record," he continued, "that I go to church every week. I'm a Catholic, and I shouldn't believe in this stuff. But it happened."

I replied that I was a Catholic, too, a former altar boy who had thought seriously about going into the priesthood. Sharing that confidence seemed to help calm him down. Then, a bit more relaxed, he began to tell his story.

In the mid-1960s, at a volunteer fire company somewhere in South Jersey, Ben Kelley, a veteran volunteer firefighter heard an emergency call broadcast over the scanner he kept on 24 hours a day in his apartment.

Less than a mile away, a man was trapped in a burning car. Ben knew the site. Since it was at an intersection between his apartment and the fire hall, Ben decided to go directly to the scene.

He arrived before any of the other company volunteers and equipment. Through the windshield glass he could see a man trapped behind the steering wheel. Flames were licking the insides of the car and victim. Hot, black smoke was pouring out from beneath the vehicle.

Disregarding his own safety, Ben put on a pair of work gloves, grabbed the hot metal handle and yanked open the driver's door.

"That's when the explosion occurred," said Chuck. "The fuel and gases trapped inside the car combined with the sudden rush of oxygen from the outside, and it created what they call a 'backdraft.' Both men were killed.

"At the autopsy, they theorized that Ben was startled from the explosion. He jumped back, but couldn't get away from the heat

7

and flames pouring out of the car. He was just sucked in by it all, consumed by the explosive blast and became part of the fireball. He was burned alive."

Chuck paused a second before going on.

"He never had a chance. His body was very badly charred . . . . Ben Kelley died at the scene. When the fire equipment arrived at the scene, there was nothing his friends could do. They found two dead bodies, one in the car and one on the pavement."

Ben Kelley's small community was shocked and touched by the tragedy. Everyone had some connection to him, through school, the church, his family or the Boy Scout troop Ben advised. The entire town closed down for the ceremonial funeral.

A trio of bagpipers came down from New York City, and more than 500 firefighters, representing states from as far away as Ohio, New Hampshire and North Carolina marched in the solemn funeral procession.

The coffin bearing Ben Kelley's body was carried atop a pumper truck and, as it passed the town firehouse, the siren blew. It was "sounding the last alarm" that firefighter Ben Kelley would answer as the procession slowly snaked its way toward the town cemetery.

At the next annual meeting, the fire company board of directors, with support from the township and state volunteers committee, erected a bronze plaque and a memorial photograph in the fire station hallway in honor of Ben Kelley. Over the years, every new class of recruits was told the story of the late firefighter's heroic rescue attempt during their training sessions.

About 1980, nearly 15 years after the tragic accident, the fire station was doubled in size. A newer, larger section housed the fire trucks and the expanded administrative offices. The bay area that formerly housed pumper trucks was used for the ambulance crews. The old offices were gutted and a recreation room was built on that site, for the volunteers who spent a lot of time on standby status at the station.

But the Ben Kelley memorial area, complete with plaque and picture, remained in the hallway of the old building.

"I don't know exactly when it started," Chuck said. "I was there from 1965 to 1988. They say it always happened in the same area, only in the old firehouse sections of the building. And the few times it went into the hallway that connects to the new wing, the sounds never went past the Ben Kelley memorial. It's as if they stopped dead when they reached that point."

Chuck spoke of a single pair of footsteps in the hall.

"It didn't matter whether you were in the rec room alone or with someone else. Someone would turn their head or stop talking and say, 'Do you hear that?' At first one person noticed the sounds, then others.

"Eventually, it got to the point where we were always listening for the footsteps. Then, when we heard them, we would all look at the door, waiting for someone to walk into the room. But no one ever came in, and the steps just stopped, like somebody was standing and waiting, in the hall outside the doorway.

"It was driving us crazy. Later, when we heard the walking, we would run, I mean charge for the door, as fast as we could, to pull it open to see who was out in the hall. But there never was anyone there. I mean never."

Chuck said on some nights one person would be assigned to sit near the door and wait for the footsteps, so he could yank it open the very second that they stopped.

That, too, turned up absolutely nothing.

Chuck was getting into the story now, and I had to slow him down to catch up with my notes. During the pause he asked, "Am I doing okay? You don't think I'm crazy, do you?"

I smiled, shook my head, and he picked up his notes and gave a quick smile.

"My parents won't let me tell them about this, and my wife won't listen either, so this is good for me to get this off my chest," he added.

I nodded, explaining that I've heard the same statement from dozens of others. I could see he felt better realizing there were others who acted and felt as he did.

"You have to understand," he continued, "that all this activity only happened in the old wing. Never in the new sections. Sometimes, we'd go through the entire firehouse—checking every room, looking in every closet and storage area, even searching the stalls in the men's and women's rooms—to see if anyone other than those of us in the rec room was there. We were sure no one else was in that building but us, and still the footsteps came . . . and then disappeared."

9

There were a few other things that bothered the firefighters, including:

• A "cold spot" that occurred sometimes in front of the Ben Kelley memorial plaque;

• The sound of something invisible breathing just outside the recreation room door; and

• The mysterious swinging of the long cord, dangling from the pay phone, located in the hallway between the Kelley memorial site and the door to the recreation area.

"All this went on for years, I mean a long time," Chuck said. "It was driving us crazy. We never found anybody playing a practical joke on us. We never found anybody in the building, and we never saw anything. No clouds of mist or smoke or spooky shapes floating in the halls. Nothing was ever damaged. The TV never went on or off by itself. No classic haunting stuff, other than the footsteps and cold spot."

A tight smile crossed Chuck's face when he recalled the evening a friend of his was visiting at the firehouse. At one point, Chuck left his friend alone in the rec room and went out to answer the phone that was ringing in the hall.

"When I came back," Chuck recalled, "he was standing up and looking around. He told me he swore he heard footsteps in the doorway and had been wondering why the person didn't come in. He also said, while he was looking at the door, that he had the feeling that someone was with him, right beside him, in the room. But, obviously, there was no one there. No one that we could see, anyway."

Chuck said the newer volunteers who had not known Ben Kelley were careful not to talk about the incidents around the older guys who had been at the station when the firefighter met his accidental death. Even 15 or 20 years after the tragedy, some of his close friends got teary eyed and would leave the room when any discussion about Ben Kelley began.

"It was a touchy situation," Chuck said. "Some people were scared to be alone in the station, and others thought it was kind of neat.

"But everybody, from the oldest member to the newest recruit, knew about the unexplained incidents. Some believed in them and others didn't, or at least they said they didn't. But there were a number of members who knew Ben and who didn't want his memory trashed by people who thought his ghost was running loose around the firehouse.

10

"I knew Ben in passing, we weren't in the same training class, I came on board a few years after him. Personally, his ghost being there wouldn't have bothered me. But among the old timers, me and his good friend, T.J., were in the minority about that."

In 1988, not too long before Chuck left the station and moved to Delaware, he, T.J. and six other regulars who called themselves the "Crazy Eight" decided they had to do something. The ongoing mystery was driving all of them crazy,

"We had to be careful," Chuck said. "We couldn't have a priest come in and exorcise the place, because nobody from the outside was allowed into the firehouse. It was against club rules to have anything done without board approval. We could be dismissed, especially for something they'd consider goofy, like this."

Ralph, one of the younger guys, mentioned he had a Ouija board and offered it as a possible solution to their problem. But, Chuck recalled, the suggestion generated an immediate stream of sarcastic comments and an equal number of disgusted looks.

"It's made by Parker Brothers," someone shouted.

"Get real," another scoffed.

"That's stupid. It's only a game," shouted somebody else, dismissing Ralph's suggestion with a wave of his hand.

But, just as they were ready to give up on the idea, someone said, *Let's give it a shot*.

"To be honest," Chuck recalled, "it was the best and only thing that we could think of. Looking back on it, I can't believe we used it. It's just a piece of wood or pressed cardboard."

While Ralph ran home to get his "toy," the other seven prepared the recreation room for the "spiritual" session. It was late, about 10 o'clock on a weekday night. No one else usually came in at that time, so the Crazy Eight figured, timing wise, it was a good opportunity. During the proceedings, a person was assigned to each doorway, to give a signal in case anyone else arrived. That would give the others time to hide the board under the couch. Someone else got a pen and paper to record the letters and figure out the board's responses—if there were any.

Chuck was one of the two people selected to work the board and move the "planchette," or *pointer* as Chuck referred to it, with his fingertips.

T.J., Ben's good friend, agreed to ask the questions.

"We figured if it was one of us, we'd feel more comfortable hearing the questions from someone we knew. That's why we picked T.J.

Spirits Between the Bays

"I sat there, totally embarrassed, with my knees touching a guy named Lenny," Chuck said. "And I thought to myself this is the stupidest thing I've ever done in my life. Everybody else gathered around watching. You could tell that some of them were serious and hoping something would happen. The rest of us thought it was just plain stupid, like a bunch of third graders secretly playing talk to the ghost in someone's attic.

"My fingertips were barely touching the pointer when T.J. asked the first question: *Is there anyone here who would like to talk to us?*

"I swear, I felt the thing start to move and get warmer. I was so surprised that I let go of it and it stopped. Everybody was shouting that I was kidding, but I wasn't. The pointer was moving and my hands were shaking. I had to take a minute to calm down. I looked at Lenny. Neither of us had pushed it and, slowly, we began again."

The second time T.J. asked: "*Is there anybody here who would like to talk to us?*" and the glass circle crawled along and stopped over the word "*Yes.*"

The next question was: "*Do you stay here?*"

"*Yes*"

"*Do you like us?*"

"*Yes.*"

"*Do you go out on calls with us?*"

"*Yes.*"

"*Do you try to protect us?*"

"*Yes.*"

Chuck paused, taking a break from his story.

We had been talking for about 45 minutes in the restaurant, and I could tell he was beginning to get a little excited. The memories of the event obviously were vivid and still affected him after nearly eight years.

We took a break, ordered another round and, after he downed a healthy swallow, he was ready to continue his story.

He remembered that the people circled around the board, watching him, had serious doubts about what was happening. Some of them knelt on the floor, to get their eyes level with the planchette, to see if either Chuck or Lenny was pushing it along to make up the answers.

"I swear, our fingertips were hardly making contact with the movable thing," Chuck said. "And, in the beginning, the pointer was moving very slow. After a while, though, the thing was flying across the board, especially when it was spelling out answers. People were shouting out the letters to the person taking notes.

T.J. asked the spirit: *"Do you like the fire house?"*

"Yes."

"Why don't you go to the new section of the firehouse?'

"N-o-t-m-i-n-e."

"Why are you here?"

"H-o-m-e."

Finally, T.J. asked: *"Ben, is that you?"*

"I swear, I will remember that moment forever! The pointer immediately went straight to 'Yes.' But it moved so fast that I thought it was going to fly right off the board. But then it felt like somebody hit the brakes on a car real hard, just before going over a cliff. It stopped dead above the 'Yes.'

"But T.J. still wasn't convinced, and he started to laugh and make comments like: 'Nice trick' and 'No way.' He said he was tired of fooling around and decided to ask the spirit a question that only he and Ben knew the answer to.

"T.J. said, 'If it's really you, Ben, tell me what your favorite thing to do is.'

"None of us knew the answer, so we couldn't fake it even if we wanted to. The pointer spelled out the letters '1-R-D.' Over and over it kept going back to '1-R-D,' '1-R-D,' repeating those letters and that number, at least four or five times. T.J., meanwhile, started nodding. Apparently, he knew the answer.

"We're all waiting, wondering what it could be. 'Reading,' someone suggested. "Big Red 1' another person shouted. The rest were totally unsure of what the message might mean.

"Confused, tired and impatient, Lenny and I lifted our fingers off the pointer, but we kept them hovering over it, since we figured we'd be continuing the questions in a few moments.

"At the same time, T.J. said, 'Do you mean you want to go out and *Have one for the road?'* referring to Ben's habit of saying, *'Let's all go out and have one for the road.'*

"But when Ben and the guys went out, T.J. explained to us later, they'd be out drinking all night long, and the next day they'd all laugh about how long 'one for the road' with Ben would last."

Chuck said as soon as T.J. spoke the words "one for the road," the pointer shot across the board toward the printed word "Yes." It was moving so fast, that it flew off the edge of the board and landed on the floor.

"But," Chuck said, looking up from his notes, his voice totally serious and low, "There was nobody touching it . . . . We didn't have our fingertips on the damn thing. It just took off on its own power across the 'Yes' word."

Chuck leaned back against the booth. His story practically over. He looked as exhausted as he said he had been at the end of that night working the Ouija board.

I waited for him to finish. He took another sip of his beer, then put his arms back on the table. Leaning forward he continued.

"T.J. became useless after that. He stopped laughing and started to cry. I remember, he just fell into a corner of the sofa, put his head down and sobbed. Somebody else tried to ask it a few questions, but no one had any heart for it after what had just happened. We were all physically drained and packed it up."

Chuck said that one of the most unusual things occurred the next night, when the Crazy Eight met as usual in the rec room of the firehouse. No one said a single word about the previous night.

"It was crazy," he said, shaking his head. "We just looked at each other, and no one said a word. We all knew we were thinking about it, but not one person wanted to bring it up."

It's been more than 20 years since Ben Kelley's death, and eight years since that night with the Ouija board. Sometimes the events cross Chuck's mind, when he's picking up people who have been in a car wreck, or when he's on a fire scene. Flashes of thoughts even appear when he sees a firetruck pass by on the street or hears a siren.

The images come quickly, in bursts and disappear. He can deal with it, he said. But he still doesn't have a good, steady handle on that night, mainly because it's both unbelievable and real.

"You see," Chuck said, "I was there and it happened to me. If I heard the story I just told you, my first reaction would be that someone was pulling my chain, making it up. But that would have been before I had the experience myself. Now . . . well, I'd say now I'm open to a lot more.

"I will admit, though, that I'm not scared of the spirit or whatever it was that occurred that night. I'd walk back into that building alone, right now. I'd even stay there late at night. And if anything happened, I'd just know it was Ben Kelley, coming back for a visit."

Now that he's sampled a taste of the unknown, would Chuck ever want to go through it again?

He answered the question without the slightest pause, as if he'd thought about it often.

"I always believed there was something other than us, something more out there than what we can see," he said. "It's something I'm glad I experienced. I don't know if it's a thrill or a quest for knowledge. But, in total truth, I definitely would go anywhere, at anytime, to experience it again."

Apparently satisfied that he had gotten through the story, Chuck smiled, held his glass up signaling a toast, and tossed back his head and emptied the glass.

We sat in silence for a less than a minute when his wife appeared. Perfect timing, I thought.

The two full shopping bags dangling from her wrists indicated that she, too, had had a fruitful day.

I stood up, shook Chuck's hand, said my good-byes and watched the couple head outside.

As he was holding the restaurant door open for his wife, Chuck turned to look back in my direction. I waved, thinking he was offering a final gesture of farewell. Then he shouted, "I called T.J. the other day."

I was confused.

Half of the word "What" escaped my lips.

Then he added, "*He's* still there," and he turned, walked out the door and headed toward the beach.

About the Ouija Board

The Ouija board derives its name from two foreign words for "Yes"—the French "Oui" and the German "Ja." The heart-shaped triangular device that is used to point out the letters or numerals printed on the board is called a "planchette."

Author's notes:

•While attending Salesianum School, an all-male Catholic high school in Wilmington, Delaware, in the early 1960s, a priest of the faculty told us about a colleague who was doing research on Ouija boards.

The priest had left the board out of its box one night on the desk near his bed. He was awakened in early morning darkness to discover the planchette, moving on its own power in a circular motion across his chest. He promptly boxed up the "game" and suddenly, but understandably, lost interest in that research project and focused on something a bit less threatening.

Spirits Between the Bays

•A Ouija board was a regular source of amusement in Adolph's Cafe, my family's neighborhood beer garden in Wilmington, Delaware. My sisters, cousins and other regulars who used it each Friday night claimed to have contacted deceased relatives and passing souls.

One of the more unusual contacts was made with a former nun, who had apparently lived at the nearby St. Hedwig's School convent. A check, made during the next week, discovered her name in records dating back to the 1920s. She was deceased and no one in the family had ever heard the name before it appeared during that passing visit one Friday evening on our bar's Ouija board.

The bar board was officially retired soon afterwards during another interesting contact. In the midst of the questioning of an unknown spirit, several shelves—that had been securely attached to the walls—left their proper place of residence and flew across the room, leaving a number of broken objects in their wake.

•Professional medium Genevieve Alexander, of Newark, Delaware, told me during an interview, "I don't have anything to do with Ouija boards. They are the most dangerous of all the items associated with the occult. Using one is like taking the microphone of a tape recorder, turning it on and placing it out on a street corner. You leave yourself open to anything passing by that wants to come along and come inside. I recommend that people destroy them completely. Don't simply throw it out in the trash, because someone else may come along and decide to use it. They should be destroyed."

'I Thought We Had a . . . .'

Firefighters and emergency ambulance personnel know what it's like to be hit with an adrenaline rush, experience the horrifying state of fear and stare death in the eye.

Their job is to wait for tragedy to make the first move, then try to respond and save those who often are just a few weak breaths away from that permanent state of death. Since no one knows when an emergency will occur, firefighters spend a lot of time listening for the bell to ring.

Passing hours upon hours waiting for bad news is a tough way to spend one's life. During that time, emergency personnel talk family, share snapshots, swap war stories and, generally, shoot the breeze. It doesn't take too many 12-hour shifts to learn a lot about the people who back you up in life threatening situations.

Over the years, many volunteers come to think of their firehall as a second—or even a first—home.

Reds Abel loved his firehouse—the smell, the sounds, the people, even the air he breathed while walking in the wide open bays that housed the gleaming red, powerful fire engines.

He had spent 15 years as a volunteer firefighter in New Castle County, Delaware. When he moved downstate about 10 years ago, the first thing he did—even before he unpacked his belongings and moved into his new home—was sign up as a volunteer.

"My wife couldn't believe it," Reds said, smiling. "She said I was crazy to leave her home with the crates and boxes and furniture coming, to go check out the firehall. But," he added with a laugh, "none of the guys down at the firehouse thought there was anything strange about it."

Over the years, Reds had earned a reputation. If anyone needed a job done, he was always ready, willing and 'Abel.'

Spirits Between the Bays

Reds admitted that he had seen a lot of things as a volunteer. Death, injury, close calls, and a lot of crazy incidents that provided a good supply of laughs.

But, he added, in the early 1980s when he was at a previous firehouse, he almost encountered a ghost.

"Marge, my wife, actually saw it," Reds said. "Me, I wasn't that lucky—or unlucky, as the case may be—but I came pretty close."

Firefighters usually sit in the recreation room during their shift. In the summer or spring, you'll see some of them waiting around the benches, outside in front of the building, having a smoke or two. But the main gathering spot for conversation and camaraderie is the rec room.

Usually, the TV is on, a few guys are playing checkers and a half-dozen others are talking or reading the paper.

Reds spent almost 10 years at this particular station and, during that time, he recalled hearing footsteps and doors opening and closing when no one else was supposed to be in the building.

"In the beginning, the first few times it happened to me, I ignored it," Reds said. "Nobody else sitting in the room seemed to be bothered. But then, one night, I asked, 'Did you hear that door open and close? Is somebody else here?' And one of the other guys looked up and said, real casual, 'That's just *him* visiting.' They just talked it off like nothing."

A veteran member eventually explained to Reds that an older member had died in the recreation room years before. Firehouse legend is that the dead man's spirit haunts the building in rather unique ways.

Reds was told that sometimes a shape or figure would be seen in the rec room, sitting in a chair. But when anyone took a second glance the shape would be gone.

As far as spectres from the beyond were concerned, everyone agreed that the disappearing act and foot-steps were pretty common stuff. But the ghost's pranks eventually became a bit more bothersome when he became more active.

Reds was on duty one night when the alarm sounded. The volunteers in the building jumped into their gear and prepared the trucks as other firefighters arrived from home, leaving their cars parked in a crazy, scattered pattern all over the lot.

Reds explained that the officer of each truck sits in the passenger seat, next to the driver

During this alarm, Reds heard the officer yell, "Let's move it!" and Reds immediately jumped onto the back platform of the truck, expecting it to take off any second.

After holding onto the bar and waiting a full minute, which in an emergency situation can seem like an hour, Reds ran along the right side of the truck toward the front and shouted up to the officer, "Are we going or not?"

"The officer," Reds recalled, "looked down at me, real odd like, and said, 'Well, I thought we had a driver. That's why I told everybody to get on . . . . But we don't.'

"When he ran toward the truck, the officer said he saw, as clear as day, a driver at the wheel. But when he got inside, the driver's seat was empty."

A few days later, Reds was home when an alarm came over the scanner he keeps on in the kitchen. His wife, Marge, rode with him to the station.

"I rushed out of the car and ran inside to get my equipment," Reds said. "While my wife was in the parking lot, she looked up and saw someone in the truck's driver's seat. But later, she said it scared her, because when she looked up just a few seconds later, he was gone.

"When we came back in after the fire, my wife talked to an officer in the company. She described the guy she saw, who was in plain clothes, not a uniform. When she was done, the officer, who knew the man who had died, told her she had described his dead friend to a T."

Reds shook his head and paused when he was asked to explain his thoughts, his feelings about the strange firehouse incidents.

"I don't know what to think. I don't know what to say," he said, softly. Then, after a few seconds, he added, "I can't be sure of one thing or another. I do know it happens. I heard the door and the footsteps. My wife, I believe what she said she saw."

Changing the subject slightly, Reds continued his explanation, "I had a

dream about my uncle two days after he died. He was in the same suit they buried him in. He stood in front of me and said, 'Don't worry. I'm okay.'

"I don't know if it was my subconscious getting the best of me—or really him. I like to think there's something to it.

"I believe the officer saw the ghost driver that day. We have sat in that rec room and heard the footsteps, the doors. It wasn't from the air conditioner or heater turning on or off. The steps were too damn close for anyone to be able to run off without us catching them."

Then, Reds reinforced his earlier comments, referring to the firehouse as a very special place, a second home, for those that get it in their system.

"The guys who belong are dedicated," he added. "I don't know what it is, but it affects us. Maybe that's what brings him back from the great beyond. Some people belong to clubs where they can relax. It's their place. Maybe, in this case, the firehouse is his little place of heaven."

Pausing, then beaming a bright smile, Reds added, "I hope when I die, I can come back and stay at the firehouse, too. That way I can make up for all the time that my wife won't let me stay there now."

Abigail

R ay and Sharon sat at either end of the rectangular table in the restored country kitchen. Their farmhouse is located north of Middletown, Delaware, not far from the north-to-south portion of the Mason Dixon Line that marks the boundary between the First State and the Free State of Maryland.

Thick, varnished oak planks from an old barn that stood on the property contrast with the room's bright white plaster walls and new, modern appliances. Through the doorway one could see parts of the renovated parlor, located in the oldest section of the house that dates back to the early 1700s.

Heat and the crackling of dry wood reached across the room from the kitchen fireplace. It was cold outside, overcast. Dark fall clouds moved fast, pushed by the force of the gusting wind. A perfect setting to talk about ghosts.

Soon after the interview started, it became apparent that Ray, a school teacher, and Sharon, a travel agent, had experienced unexplained events years earlier, when they lived in New Jersey.

"We've always lived in old places," Sharon said, "and I don't have any explanation for what happens, or why things seem to happen to us. But they do."

About 15 years ago, while living on an estate in Red Bank, New Jersey, Ray helped carry out the body of a man from the main bedroom of the manor house where he had died. Later, the new owner invited Ray and Sharon to move in the home and fix it up, rent free.

"It was what I like to do," Ray said, "so it seemed like a great deal. We stayed there about five years and completely redid the place.

"One night, while I was working in one of the rooms, all of the lights and electricity went out. Totally. Everything," he said.

21

Spirits Between the Bays

After returning from the basement—which friends and even the family dog refused to ever enter—Ray found his wife standing in the dark parlor, pointing to a sliver of yellow light coming from under the doorway of the main bedroom.

"I swear that house was haunted," Sharon said. "All the electricity was out in every single part of the house . . . except the main bedroom where that man had died."

Ray said he had checked the breakers, plus the fuses for the older section, and everything was in order. There was no logical reason for the lights to be off. Plus, if they were out, there was no reason that they should still be on in only that one room.

There also is the story of the leaves, which really bothers Ray but causes Sharon to laugh.

Apparently, the man who had died in the estate house was a very neat person, and he spent a large amount of time outside cleaning his yard.

One autumn weekend, when Ray and Sharon arrived home from shopping, there were at least 30 small piles of leaves, resting in little mounds across the entire yard.

"There was no rake, no sign of anyone around," Sharon said. "But the leaves were there."

"His yard was always spotless," said Ray, "and there we were, looking at all these little piles of raked leaves. I really hate that, because you have to go around and pull them all together into larger mounds to pick up. I said to myself, 'Who the hell did that?'

"We never found out. If anyone we know did it, they haven't admitted it after all these years. The electricity going out and staying on in that room, that only happened once. But between the leaf piles and the electric problems, plus that guy dying there, all that was enough for me," Ray said.

A few years later, they moved into an old farmhouse in Holmdale, New Jersey.

A large Catholic family with seven children had lived in the home for years. They were very devout in their faith and had a large number of religious objects and hangings on display. For some reason, when they moved they left behind a framed picture of the Blessed Virgin Mary.

As Ray started to fix up the home, he took the picture off of the hallway wall and placed it in the back of a nearby closet for safe keeping.

22

"It had signatures of all of the children on it," Ray recalled, "and I thought they might come back for it. I don't know why they would have left it. I didn't want to throw it out, so I saved it for whomever might come to get it."

For years the image of the Blessed Virgin lived on the floor of the hall closet. No one remembered she was there. No one took her out into the light of day.

In 1992, when Ray and Sharon were moving to their present home in Middletown, Delaware, they packed up their belongings and made several trips to unload.

"When I returned to the house in Jersey to pick up the final stuff for the last run," Ray said, "the picture, that was in the closet all those seven years, was back on the wall—in the exact spot where I found it years before.

"I had the only key to the door. The owner didn't even have a house key, so no one could have gotten in. Even if they did, how would they have known to find it and then hang it on the exact place I had found it?

"I left it hanging there and didn't touch it, locked the door and left. That was a weird one."

As soon as Ray finished the story, Sharon nodded, grinned, then started singing the *Twilight Zone* theme: "Do-do-do-do. Do-do-do-do."

"She does that a lot," Ray said, pointing across the table, "probably because she thinks I'm crazy, since I've started reading a lot of books about ghosts."

Shifting the focus to their present homestead, Ray passed me a thick photo album that was resting on the kitchen table. It contained interior and exterior shots of their home in various stages of neglect, disrepair, restoration and completion.

Having done some research, the couple knew that their land and house had been one of 14 farms in Delaware and Maryland owned by the Bradys, a family instrumental in the construction of the nearby Chesapeake and Delaware Canal.

For 100 years prior to their arrival in 1992, Ray and Sharon said the farmhouse they now own had been occupied by a number of different tenants. Dark paneling covered the original walls, ceilings were caving in, the roof leaked, the out buildings were practically falling down.

To anyone riding by, the structure was an excellent candidate for a Halloween haunted house.

When they moved in during August, Ray decided to complete one room at a time. His goal was to finish the living room in time for Christmas. Among other things, that involved stripping the walls and putting on a coat of new plaster.

In mid November, he had nearly completed the entire room. The last area to be plastered was the center section of one living room wall, directly above the hearth of the fireplace. Ray said he finished it off by 11 o'clock one night and went to bed, figuring the walls would be dry and the room ready to paint the next day.

In the morning he noticed that an 8-inch-square section of plaster had fallen from the left front of the fireplace, above the mantle, and landed on the floor.

"It was odd," said Ray, "out of the whole room, this was the only spot that didn't take. I went back that night, scratched the original wall down, warmed it up with a heat lamp to get ready, and repatched it.

"The next morning, the same spot was messed up and the plaster was gone again. I was really getting mad at that point. As I started preparing the surface again, I called my wife and we both looked at it real close."

They discovered the name *Abigail Brumm*, written three times in tiny, flowery script in different spots of the exposed section of old wall. Ray said the name had been carved into the original surface—meaning it had to have been signed when the original coat of plaster was applied and drying, more than 200 years ago.

"This was really getting strange," Ray said, "and I was getting a creepy feeling about it. I asked myself: *Why would it only fall out in this one section?* There was no reason, all of the rest of the room held fine."

Sharon, offering a "Do-do-do-do, Do-do-do-do," said she thought it was funny at the time, but her husband was really getting aggravated. "I said maybe somebody's trying to send a message."

Ray agreed, "I think Abigail put her name in it and wanted somebody to see it, and I did, when I was plastering. When I told my mother and brother about it, they came over to see. They said I should just leave it alone, not plaster it over and put a frame around it. But I was trying to get the room to look right."

Later that night, Ray tried to fix the area a third time. But, like his two previous efforts, the new plaster did not hold and the name *Abigail Brumm* appeared again, staring at Ray the following morning.

"I decided, that was it," Ray said "I'm not plastering any more. I'm drywalling the center part of the chimney. And I did. After that, I thought I was done with it. But there's more to the story, a part I didn't even connect with Abigail immediately."

Ray said that the drywall went up on Thursday, completing the preparation for the painting of the room. Late Saturday morning, when he was out in the yard walking his dog, a car came up the driveway and a woman got out.

She asked Ray if he knew anything about the history of his house.

"I asked her, 'Why?' and she said, 'You're going to think I'm nuts, and my husband doesn't know I'm here, but . . . .' "

Ray waited out the pause, and the unexpected visitor said that her husband told her not to tell anyone what had happened. But she couldn't keep it to herself.

She explained to Ray that her husband, that morning, was in the driveway of their newly built home, which was nearby. While on the ground, changing the oil in their car, the man looked up and saw a woman standing above him. She looked eerie and was staring down at him.

The ghostly woman was dressed in late 1700s-style, Colonial clothing. As the Saturday morning mechanic got up to talk to her, she disappeared right in front of his eyes.

"I listened to the woman, who was standing and talking to me in my driveway," Ray said, "but I said to myself, 'Yeah! Right!'

"She told me she came to our place because it was the old farmhouse of the area and, apparently, the original owners had owned all the land, including the property that her house was on. She wanted to know if I could tell her anything at all. She said she might do some research on the house, but we never heard from her again.

"I went in and told Sharon, 'You're not going to believe this.' To both of us, it sounded like it was *Twilight Zone* stuff."

Taking her cue, Sharon offered a quick "Do-do-do-do," before adding, "Maybe it was Abigail and we released her from the wall. Maybe she was trying to get out and we let her out. I guess the drywall covering won't keep her trapped inside anymore."

Ray leaned back in his kitchen chair, thinking about the events.

"At first, I was just annoyed and didn't think it was anything paranormal or ghostly. I was just upset about having to keep doing the same thing over and over, trying to get the room done by Christmas. But, when that woman came to the yard with that story—just a few days after the plaster was falling out and we found the name—that was weird.

"I know this place is old. We found one brick with the year 1799 carved into it, but I know the house is a lot older than that. They used to keep slaves up in the third floor servant's quarters, in the attic. There were orchards here where the slaves used to work. We've found remnants of back and side stairways. I've always been interested in old houses, and I enjoy fixing them up."

Sharon said they have not had any unusual experiences since the fall of 1992, when the plaster fell and the neighbor came up the driveway with her ghostly story.

"But," Sharon added, "I don't really like it up on the third floor. I do my work up there, in my office, during the day. But I get odd feelings quite a bit. You can almost sense the whole house is moving in the wind sometimes, and at night . . . . Well, there were those slaves that lived up in those rooms. It just gives you a chill when you think about all the things that may have happened here."

Ray laughed, adding at least Abigail helped them name a member of the family.

"Our dog had puppies soon after the plastering incidents. We decided Abigail was a nice old-fashioned name, and nobody uses it anymore. So we named one of our dogs after her. Apparently, she doesn't mind. At least we haven't heard from her about it . . . yet."

Bigfoot in Maryland?

For decades, stories about Bigfoot, North America's version of the Himalayan Abominable Snowman, have appeared at irregular intervals in supermarket tabloids, as well as in more reputable newspapers and magazines.

While a vast majority of the sightings since the early 1900s have occurred in the Pacific Northwest, there have been reports of hairy, ape-like Sasquatch beings throughout the United States. Interestingly, more than a few unexplained footprints and, in a some cases, sightings have occurred in the state of Maryland.

Bob Chance—an environmental scientist, naturalist and former high school science teacher from the Darlington area of Harford County, Maryland—stumbled upon a possible Bigfoot incident in 1972. Since that time, he has been involved in researching other incidents in Eastern Maryland related to the tall, nocturnal, ape-like creature.

We sat in the studio of Chance's historic Colonial home, in the quaint Village of Berkley, surrounded by arrowhead displays, colorful turtle shells, framed butterflies, stuffed owls, tropical fish, an extensive natural science library and photographs from his travels on other continents. At a thoughtful, relaxed pace, the soft-spoken founder and former director of the Susquehannock Environmental Center shared some of the more unusual experiences that have occurred during his ongoing, 24-year investigation.

In the spring of 1972, Chance was leading a high school canoe trip in Muddy Creek, Pennsylvania, on the Susquehanna River about 15 miles north of his home.

One of the canoes had become lodged under a waterfall and he and several students spent some time recovering it from the rocky gorge. Close to sunset, as the group was walking back to the truck through the forest, a 30-lb. rock landed in front of them. It came from the ridge above. Soon, another rock of similar size and weight landed nearby, recalled Chance. One of the rocks struck a student in the shoulder, and Chance and the rest of the party shouted at the unseen assailant.

Running to the top of the ridge, the group sensed that an animal or person was very close. They decided to take the injured student to the hospital rather than pursue their attacker. But, as they walked toward the truck another rock was tossed in their direction.

Chance wondered who or what may have tried to attack or harm them . . . or keep them away. He thought it probably was a person, or maybe a deer that had accidentally dislodged the rocks as it ran across the ridge.

About 18 months after the rock throwing incident, while attending a conference on the Sasquatch, Chance discovered a possible answer. Participants discussed the secretive creature's tendency to throw things, at irregular intervals, in the direction of those who approached.

"I didn't know much about the creature's habitat or behavioral pattern at the time," Chance said. But he discovered that at other sightings the animal had been known to throw things at intruders.

Over the years, his interest in Bigfoot continued, and he periodically visited isolated watersheds throughout Harford County, checking out reports of unexplained incidents.

Being called to examine a trail of very large footprints in the snow during the winter of 1978 near Delta, Pennsylvania, increased Chance's belief that there might be a mid-Atlantic version of Bigfoot in Maryland.

By the late '70s, Chance said he had investigated—in person or by phone—more than 20 sightings. At that time, combining what he had learned with the subsequent incidents, Chance began to think the rock throwing that occurred years earlier in Muddy Creek may have been caused by a passing Sasquatch.

As of early 1996, his slim folder had grow to contain 104 incidents, most within a 25-mile radius of his home. Generally, his area of research extends from the Gunpowder Falls in the southwest to Muddy Creek in the north, Deer Creek and Broad Creek in the south and the Octoraro region in Cecil County to the east.

"I've talked to raccoon hunters and farmers, hikers and deer hunters," he said. "They've told me of their missing livestock, about hearing screams, smelling strong odors and they described these huge tracks they've seen. Over the years, I've gotten a sense of what the animal's feeding patterns are, plus its intelligence, its curiosity and its instinctive ability to avoid detection."

After talking with other researchers in different parts of the world, in British Columbia and Washington state, Chance developed a list of factors that would make it difficult, or even impossible for Bigfoot to exist in the East. These included: the dense population, lack of a large undeveloped/forested area and topography that did not help concealment.

"I wondered why one of the creatures hadn't been wounded by a car or sighted by deer hunters or seen going through people's garbage. Even if it's nocturnal, there should be someone who has seen one. I'm still wondering about these things. Even though I've never seen it, I still can't stop the quest."

Never far from Chance's thoughts are the tracks. It always seems to come back to markings in the snow. Similar to the Delta, Pennsylvania, footprints in 1978, significant sets of very large tracks appeared in the winter of 1995.

A sudden February snowfall provided evidence of a very large creature that seemed to travel the length of Harford County and headed from southeast to northwest into Pennsylvania. During that excursion through the area, at least six families reported footprints or late evening sightings of some kind of a large creature near their farms or homes on a single winter evening.

Remnants of the tracks indicated a three-toed creature with 15-inch feet and up to a 70-inch stride.

"I hadn't much to go on for about 10 years," Chance said. "That series of events was quite significant."

Over the years, Chance has earned himself a reputation as the area's foremost Bigfoot hunter. Telephone calls to his home reporting unusual incidents are not uncommon. In addition to footprints, people have reported high-pitched shrieking.

"They've been described as wails with various levels of amplitude," Chance said. "I've heard the sounds, both in the outdoors and on tape recordings. It's almost like a shrill whistle, but it can end in a roar. It's as if it comes from a chest cavity of tremendous proportions."

In 1977, in Deer Creek Valley, Chance said a woman discovered large tracks in her garden. One night, all the dogs in the neighborhood charged out after the unseen monster. One dog never returned. It was found swinging from a tree, 10 feet above the ground with its neck broken.

"Most dogs cower in fear from the scent," said Chance. "It's like sewage or sulfur or rotten eggs. I've heard it described as smelling like rotting meat. Some say it emits an odor when cornered or approached, like a skunk."

In a few instances, witnesses have told Chance they've noticed the creature staring in house windows, apparently fascinated with the passing images on televisions.

He said he has read reports that similar traits have been displayed by gorillas in zoos.

Chance smiled as he mentioned that he gets some odd looks when strangers realize he has more than a passing interest in Bigfoot. The reaction can range from aloofness and ridicule to a desire to accompany him on the hunt.

"A lot of people want to be in on the actual research," he said. "I practically always turn them down. Some of them have actually seen something themselves, and they want reinforcement in their own minds.

"But I usually go alone, with a tape recorder and camera. Sometimes I take my dogs. The more people involved reduces the chances of an encounter, since the animal can sense the intrusion."

In two instances, Chance believes he has been close to an encounter with the creature of his quest. One was near a garbage dump behind a trailer close to Deer Creek.

"I pulled down the driveway at dusk," he recalled. "I heard tremendous thrashing. Whatever it was ran right through the tree saplings at a high rate of speed. The next day I returned and took some plaster casts of the footprints.

"People ask me if I've ever been scared, and my answer is 'Yes.' I was definitely scared when rocks, double the size of a football, were being thrown.

"Still, I'll go into abandoned stone shells or ruins that used to be barns or homes. I have this image of the animal, standing flush against the wall in the darkness. I don't think it will hurt me. I hope it realizes I'm not aggressive and mean no harm."

After reviewing more than 100 local reports, Chance has some opinions on the physical characteristics of the creature:
- Nearly 7 feet tall, weighing 350-500 lbs.
- Extremely long arms
- Sloped cranium
- Barrel chest
- Very large mid section
- No neck
- Flat nose
- Reddish to brown to salt-and-pepper hair

Regarding its habits:
- There are significantly fewer, probably 100 to 200, in the Eastern corridor than the larger numbers in the West,
- They travel in three- or five-member groups or, in the case of males, alone,
- A half-dozen use the corridor through Harford County going north in summer and south in winter,
- They winter throughout the lower Appalachians and in Alabama, Arkansas, northern Georgia and central Florida,
- They do not stay in one particular habitat and have learned to keep moving,
- They follow the ancient migratory routes of the elk, moose, deer and bear,
- They follow the river valleys and the steep slopes of the Piedmont and
- They are omnivorous, feeding on meat and vegetation.

Chance admitted that his greatest fear is that with more publicity about its presence a trophy hunter in an all-terrain vehicle would be thrilled to mount the carcass on the hood and do severe disservice to scientific study.

After more than two decades, why does Chance continues his search? After all these years, does he have an objective, a focus, something he would like to achieve?

"I want to prove the animal does exist," he said, "through photos or by witnesses' accounts. If it could be captured, I'd want to sedate it, examine it, and let it go, perhaps with a radio transmitter.

"The activity seems to come irregularly," Chance said. "The follow up doesn't take much out of me. I'll go years with nothing and then, all of a sudden the calls come in. I can't establish a pattern, but that's not a main priority.

"I'm just an amateur naturalist who has been caught up in this quest. I'm a dreamer. I'd like to think that not everything on the planet has been categorized, that there's still some pocket of natural history and wildness that hasn't yet been discovered.

"It might be there. It might not be there. It may be a bogus fairy tale I'm tracking, but I think not. Sometimes I find myself thinking that, in the future, someone will find this thing and say, 'That thing Chance was talking about 25 years ago is really out there.' "

Author's note: Anyone who has experienced an encounter or who may have information to share on the mid-Atlantic Sasquatch may write to: Bob Chance, 3631 Berkley Road, Darlington, MD 21034.

One That Got Away

For 30 years, Herb Pierce kept many of the details of this story pretty much to himself. The strange events happened a few miles south of Elkton, Maryland, in and near a small bungalow on Frenchtown Road. Herb was 17 then, and he recalled there was a good deal of excitement about the incidents at the time. But, within six months, the story was old news and interest died down.

Offering a quick smile in his living room outside Elkton in the spring of 1996, the automobile mechanic admitted that, when he had shared parts of his story, people would give him that *Are you for real?* or *What have you been drinking?* look.

He learned at an early age to keep quiet about being a major player in the theater of the bizarre.

"My cousin's husband, Frankie, who also was involved," said Herb, "well, he made the mistake of telling some guys at his work about it. Boy, I tell you, that was it. They rode him real hard. Hard enough so that he swore he wouldn't say another word about it. And he didn't. And I didn't neither."

Until now.

"Over the years," Herb explained, "I used to sit home and watch TV, and I'd see these stories about UFOs and other strange stuff on *Unsolved Mysteries* and *Sightings* and *Paranormal*. Then I would read these reports about unusual events and sightings in the newspapers. And all the time I kept thinking back to the summer of 1966, when I saw Bigfoot down on Frenchtown Road. I guess I figured it was about time now, with 30 years passing, to get the story off my chest."

At the time, Herb lived in a small cottage with Donna, his cousin, and her husband, Frank. It was a modest home, surrounded by fields of grain, and there was no telephone. To make a call, they would drive up to Route 40 and use the pay phone at Rose's Diner or one at the old Esso Truck Stop.

A few times a week, and always at night, the three residents started to hear something beating against the side of the house. Herb described it as a "big racket, like something was walking outside and fell into the side of the building. But when we went out to look, there wasn't nothing there."

Eventually, the phantom prowler began playing with a large window fan, hitting the blades and spinning them around when the fan was turned off. The residents also noticed someone or something peeking through the arch-shaped window that went across the top of the front door. Since the glass was up quite high, the prowler would have to be very tall to be able to peer through the panes.

"We had an old friend named Rick, who lived down the road," said Herb. "He was about 6 foot 8, so we accused him of being a Peeping Tom. But he said he wasn't coming around our way, and why would he want to look in on us, anyway?"

Late one evening, Herb was sitting on the back step. Frank had come home from work, run into the house and left his car running. The driver's door was open and the headlights were on.

"We had a gravel driveway," said Herb. "I heard a sound like

the car was trying to move on the gravel rocks. I'm thinking about nothing in particular, but I turn to look at the car. All of a sudden, I see this thing, about 7 feet tall. It was hairy with a face, and sort of leaning over, near the front of the car, and looking at me.

"I could see half of him. It scared me so bad that I ran into the house. I couldn't believe it. I told Donna and Frank, but by the time we all got outside it was gone. There was nothing there."

Realizing people might think Herb's story was crazy, they agreed to keep things to themselves. But, a few nights later, they all heard movement outside the house. It had returned. But this time there was a new calling card.

"I smelled it this time," Herb said. "It smelled like rotten, stinking fish odor. We were inside the house and you could smell it coming from outside. Then we heard the side of the house being hit again."

Donna drove to Route 40 and called the state police. When the officer arrived they filed a prowler complaint.

"We told him about the creature, too," said Herb. "He didn't believe it, though. Thought it was a joke."

Deciding to be prepared, Herb loaded his rifle, and Frank put shells into his double-barreled shotgun. A few weeks later, Donna and Herb went out for hamburgers. As they returned home and pulled into the driveway, they both saw it.

"There was this big, hairy creature standing in the front yard," Herb recalled. "He looked at us, and we froze. Our neighbor has a 36- or 40-inch-high fence. And this thing just walked toward it and stepped over it, without any trouble, just walking its normal stride. Donna shouted: 'We're gettin' outta here!' and she put the car in reverse. We drove to Rose's to call the state police."

When they arrived back at the house the police cruiser was in the driveway. The officer listened to their report of a hairy monster, but laughed it off as a joke.

"It was damp that night," said Herb, "so we took the officer over to look at the footprints. They were about 15 inches long and 8 inches wide. Huge. We told him to take pictures, or to make a cast. But he said there was no evidence of a crime, so he didn't do anything. He agreed to go back to the barracks and file the report as an unusual or out-of-the-ordinary incident. But I tell you, it wasn't a human footprint, and this creature, it definitely did walk on two feet."

Even though things were quiet for a while, Herb, Frank and Donna could tell the creature was about. But it made no public appearances. It seemed to keep to the shadows and offer a few tappings on the fan, sometimes peering inside through the blades and peeking in the high, front door windows.

"He'd make an effort to let you know he was around," said Herb. "We'd sort of glance at it, but not make a big fuss. We pretended we didn't see it, 'cause, in a way, we didn't really believe what we saw . . . and we couldn't explain it.

"But word got out, rumors were spreading through the whole town of Elkton about the sightings. So a bunch of teenagers from school, and other guys who lived in the area, came over at night and took turns watching for it.

"The state police were on patrol, riding around, too. One night, this trooper shot down the driveway, jumped out of his car, pulled his pistol and shouted for us to stay in the house. He ran down into the field and was gone two or three minutes. He came back and didn't say nothing. But he had a look on his face like he saw something. It was about 10 or 11 at night. He said for us not to come out and that he'd be back with a canine patrol. But he never came back that night, or the next day as far as we know."

Toward the end of the summer, a large group of amateur creature trackers met inside the house. Frank had his shotgun loaded. Herb was ready with his rifle. One guy had a pistol. Two others carried hunting knives.

"Everybody figured they needed something for self-protection," said Herb. "All the lights were off in the house. I was looking out the back door, toward the wheat field, about 40 feet away.

"It was a fairly full moon, so we could see pretty good. I saw something move in the yard. But I wasn't sure what or who it was. Now, I'd done some hunting, and I'm not going to shoot something if I don't know what it is."

After checking, Herb discovered that Frank had gone outside through the front door. In a bright white T-shirt, Frank had entered the field. Everyone waited.

After a very long two minutes had passed, the silence was broken by two quick blasts from a shotgun.

"Immediately, I heard the weirdest scream. It was a piercing scream, a cry that I'll never forget. Evidently, Frank shot this thing. Well, when he fired both barrels, I was out the back door with my rifle. Within 10 seconds, I found Frank on the ground in the wheat field. He was so scared, he was petrified to death. He had collapsed. You ever been so scared that your body freezes? Well, that's what happened to him. I leaned over and asked him if he was all right.

"He said, 'I shot it!' When I looked up, I saw it running off into the field. I ran 20 or 30 yards, and shot off 6 or 8 rounds. I didn't

36

hit it. It was dark. I was just throwing lead. I turned around and got back to Frank. He was still there. I had to pick him up and physically carry him into the house. Nobody else came out. They were inside, waiting for us to get back."

The next day the police came and, with a few of Herb and Frank's friends, explored the field. The searchers found several broken locust fence posts and mats of dark hair that were caught on a section of barbed wire.

After the trooper left, Herb and his friends went farther into the woods.

"We went into a marshy area and discovered an old neighborhood dump," said Herb. "There were two big holes, about two to three feet around. They went into the ground and looked like something you could crawl into. We all joked about who was going to go into the holes and take a look. But, we all had a feeling, a sense, that something wasn't quite right. We left . . . and that's how it ended up.

"I stayed in that house about three or four more months. But that was the last time we saw it. After that, I think it just sorta wandered off.

"I'm telling you the gospel. I admit this is hard to believe. But it happened. This was only the second or third time I've told this story. It even makes me a little nervous, after all this time, to talk about it again."

So, what does Herb think it was?

"I think it was a Bigfoot, and you'll never, ever change my mind. I saw it three or four times. I never knew anything about it, or the big size, the horrible smell. Over the years, I heard reports of sightings of big, dark, two-footed creatures in Baltimore County, Harford County, Baltimore City, over in Delaware, all across the country.

"I sat there and knew what they were. They were Bigfoots in those areas. And I'm not the only one that's seen it. At the time, back in '66, they thought we were a bunch of crazy teenagers, maybe a little drunk on alcohol. Right after it happened, I knew enough to keep quiet. Soon enough, everybody forgot about it. I figured they would."

After service in the U.S. Army and more than 25 years as a mechanic, Herb decided it was time to share his story. But, he still wants to remain anonymous.

Spirits Between the Bays

"The fact is, the story was killing me. I wanted to get it out. Maybe it will do somebody some good. I think if people read this, and they think about it, there's a possibility that other people will open up and share what happened to them.

"I want to keep some privacy, because some people think you're making it all up for fun, and the others say you're crazy. But, if I have to tell you a lie, I ain't gonna tell you nothing. That's the way I look at it. What I'm telling you is the truth. If you believe me fine. If you don't believe me, that's okay, too.

"I'll tell you this, the place out there has changed a lot over the years, lots of houses now that weren't there before. If people only knew what happened out there, I bet they'd sure be surprised."

Author's Note: In 1996, Herb ran into an old high school friend whose relatives owned a farm on Frenchtown Road, not too far from the site of Herb's old cottage. The friend said in the late 1950s, his uncles had been pestered by a hairy creature that broke into their out buildings and corn crib. On one occasion, the monster actually chased one of the farmers into the house.

According to Herb, his friend said there were quite a few more odd events that occurred in the area around Frenchtown Road, "but nobody down there wants to talk."

Snallygaster Sightings

Gorilla-Like Beast Seen Roaming Woods
Near Elkton—In Md.'s 'Snallygaster' Country

This *Washington Post* page-one headline hit the newsstands on August 28, 1953. It appeared one day after the *Cecil Whig* front-page banner below proclaimed:

'Definite Possibility' Large Monkey-Like Animal Loose,
Evidence Shows

Today, 43 years later, there are still vivid recollections, spirited talk and even some fond memories in Cecil County, Maryland, about the strange creature that was sighted but never captured.

The primary incidents are said to have taken place in a wooded farming region—just south of the Maryland-Pennsylvania line—north of the Mendenhall Crossroads, in the area of Blue Ball Road close to Nellies Corner, Blake Road and Lombardville.

Of course, the countryside has changed quite a bit during the four-plus decades since the sightings. Some of the old homesteads and out buildings have been sold and torn down. Developers have placed modern homes on a good portion of the rolling farmland. The local post office and family general stores have closed, and automobile traffic is more common than it was in the sleepy 1950s.

But remnants of the unsolved county mystery still exist. The low, block-like mushroom house—near the field where farmers H.S. Osborne and Ray "Brady" Potter reported that they sighted the hairy creature—still stands. And, perhaps more importantly, some of the actual participants in the Great Snallygaster Hunt are still around and eager to tell tales about their role in the grand search for Cecil County's Creature in the Cornfield.

Spirits Between the Bays

According to a story by reporter Don Hanes in the August 27, 1953, issue of the *Cecil Whig*: "Rumors that a gorilla or some such animal is prowling Cecil County took on strong tones of authority this week when a Lombardville farmer told how he saw the beast from a distance of 20 feet on two occasions."

Osborne reported that he had seen the creature the first time on August 12, at the edge of the cornfield only 20 feet away from his mushroom house near Lombardville. The farmer said the animal stood looking at him for "a second or two" and disappeared. It was about three in the afternoon and the day was clear with good visibility.

A week later, Osborne, along with fellow farmer Ray "Brady" Potter, saw the creature, which they described as being about 6 feet tall, standing erect, with a pink ring around its face and brownish hair. Searchers later found about 20 ears of corn, with their husks pulled back and partially eaten, scattered around a clearing in the woods.

A short time later, Joseph Eggers, who lived about a quarter-mile from Osborne, was working on a chicken house. He reported hearing a dog barking and, upon looking up, he sighted a brownish, man-sized animal that took several steps and disappeared into a cornfield.

The *Whig* reported that calls to law enforcement authorities about a gorilla-like creature had been circulating throughout the county for about a month prior to these sightings. The sheriff's office had gotten about 100 calls regarding a "prowling animal," and the game warden said his phone was "ringing constantly."

When the Osborne and Eggers reports came in, officials started to think there actually might be some unusual creature roaming out and about.

A *Whig* reporter contacted Fred Ulmer, who was curator of mammals at the Philadelphia Zoo, and conducted an interview. He indicated that, if there was a monkey-like animal in the vicinity, it probably wasn't a gorilla, because there were only two in Philadelphia and one in Baltimore. With replacement cost estimated at $50,000 each, there would have been quite an alarm if one of them had been found to be missing.

A chimpanzee was a possibility, since a full-grown chimp could reach a height of five feet. Worth only about $600, they are common in carnivals, and some are even kept as household pets. One might have escaped and be roaming the area. They could eat just about anything, including corn. However, they tend to travel and not stay in one spot. Sightings in the county indicated the beast was in the area for an extended period of time.

A Pennsylvania bear was another suggested possibility. "But," the *Whig* stated, "Osborne said he had seen bears and the beast he saw was not a bear."

The *Washington Post* article captured Osborne's and Potter's reactions to their joint sighting.

"Osborne said he told Potter to watch it and ran for his shot gun. When he got to the door and looked back, Potter was right at his heels.

" 'If you want it watched, watch it yourself,' Osborne quoted his friend. The animal was gone when they returned."

The *Whig* reported that "rumors were wild and varied about the gorilla." They included a report that a gorilla had escaped from a boat at Chesapeake City, and that another strange animal had jumped from a ship in the C. & D. Canal, but had gotten away after being shot at.

One woman said she heard that a circus train going through the county had lost two black panthers and a gorilla, and someone reported seeing the beast on the porch of the Howard House.

Farmers were keeping their shotguns handy and were warning anyone stupid enough to be roaming around dressed in a monkey suit that the situation was nothing to be monkeying around with. Many residents were prepared to shoot on sight, and parents were keeping their children close to home.

According to the *Washington Post*, the area of the sightings is believed to be the haunt of the mythical Snallygaster, a flying sea monster believed to inhabit the Chesapeake Bay and other rural and secluded valleys to the west.

❖   ❖   ❖

On a crisp March Sunday morning in 1996, Ruth Ann and Phil Johnson, his brother Doug Johnson and a neighbor who asked to remain anonymous—so we'll call him Ralph—gathered around the kitchen table at Walnut Spring Farms, off Blue Ball Road, to discuss the trio's role in the Great Snallygaster Caper of 1953.

Both the Johnsons' and Ralph's families owned farms nearby and all three men grew up together. At the time of the sightings, they lived within walking distance of the strange events and were all in their teens.

Ralph recalled heading down Blue Ball Road on a usually quiet Sunday morning and coming upon a neighbor who was shooting a pistol in the air and shouting: "There's a gorilla running around loose!"

"I thought to myself, 'That's probably nothing but one of our crazy neighbors in a bear suit,' " recalled Ralph, smiling with delight at the laughter his comment generated from the others sitting at the kitchen table.

But the Johnson brothers quickly added that what may sound funny today generated genuine concern at the time. Phone lines were buzzing, loaded shotguns were kept at the ready and landowners were patrolling their property. Sightings and rumors were the talk of the county, from Rising Sun to Chesapeake City, but particularly in the region near Lombardville, since that's where two farmers swore that they saw the gorilla-like beast.

"Word of mouth spread things pretty good," said Phil. "But you just had to go down to the Mendenhall Store at the corner to find out anything that was going on. And all the excitement was the talk of the town."

The next day, the Johnson brothers and Ralph teamed up to patrol each other's fields. With Doug and Ralph carrying loaded weapons, and Phil driving an old Jeep in the center of the formation, the trio searched the open pasture land for any sign of the monster.

"Everybody throughout the whole area was out and looking," said Doug. "We even walked up to the mushroom house where the sightings were reported and looked for tracks."

Doug added that the reports apparently generated official airplane surveillance.

"There was an airplane," he recalled, "that flew back and forth, across the whole area one entire evening. We couldn't make out the markings, so we don't know where it was from. But it was up there, right over us. Back and forth it went while we walked the fields down below. Somebody was taking this whole thing very seriously."

Phil said that recalling the excitement and activity associated with the gorilla sightings in 1953 reminded him of the 1996 reports about prowling cougars in New Castle County, Delaware, and out near New London, Pennsylvania.

He and his brother and Ralph spent several days and evenings back then searching their parcels for the elusive beast. But they didn't find anything. Nobody did.

But it sure stirred up some excitement, Phil said.

"Well, to be honest," said Ralph, "I'm just happy to be here. 'Cause if that gorilla had gotten to me I wouldn't have been able to be here eatin' and meetin' with all of you today.

"And it also taught me to be extra careful. Ever since then, I always have a shotgun ready with me when I take the top off the septic tank."

"Why's that?" someone asked.

" 'Cause you can't never tell what's gonna be down there. I heard somebody say that's where they think that gorilla or Snallygaster is still hidin' out. And if that's the case, I want to be sure that I'm prepared."

Author's note: The word "Snallygaster" is mentioned in Alyce T. Weinberg's book *Spirits of Frederick*. The term is said to be derived from the German word "schnellegeister," described as a "quick spirit, part reptile, part bird, a freak of nature."

The creature is said to have a snakelike body, viselike jaws and 25-foot-long wings, which allow it to swoop down on its prey as it emits loud screams.

In Jerome Clark's book, *Unexplained! 347 Strange Sightings, Incredible Occurrences, and Puzzling Physical Phenomena*, a chapter on "Sky Serpents" refers to a number of sightings of "enormous aerial dragons and snakes" from antiquity through the 19th century.

Obviously, the *Washington Post's* use of "Snallygaster" in its headline to describe the cause of strange events in Cecil County in 1953 was an inappropriate use of the colorful term.

The Voice

"I've never seen a ghost. But, I have to tell you, I have heard one, just as plain as you are sitting there hearing my voice, maybe plainer."

Bill Bryan, 75, was sitting on the edge of his couch, leaning forward, in an apartment in Newark, Delaware. The retiree, poet and writer took a drag on his smoke and stared at me, his expression totally serious.

His gaze was steady, his voice strong. Bill was completely sure about the details of the story he was about to share. He had thought about them for a long time—for more than six decades.

"I was about 12 years old at the time, maybe 13. Now I have to explain to you that my name is William E. Bryan. The 'E' stands for 'Elwood,' and I never liked the name Elwood. I wanted to be called Bill, because it was my first name and because it was a real boy's name.

"People would often shorten Elwood and call me Ellie. I didn't like that. My mother's name was Ella, and I just didn't want to be associated with being a girl. When I got big enough, I would punch anybody that used it. I made sure they called me Bill."

The unusual incident occurred late on a summer Saturday afternoon, while Bill was riding his bicycle. He was on his way to visit some friends who lived in his old neighborhood, racing toward the west along Front Street, in Wilmington, Delaware.

"I had just stood up on my bike, to get up more speed and to go faster and easier, rather than just sit on the seat and pedal. I was moving at a pretty good clip."

It was quiet late in the afternoon on that summer Saturday. There were not too many people around. The blocks were lined with old warehouses and shops, but they were closed. There was very little traffic. The city was getting ready to fall asleep on a hot weekend.

44

He was picking up speed, and only about five minutes from his destination.

"Suddenly," Bill recalled, "this voice shouted from up over my right shoulder. It sounded like it came from the direction of an empty block, or out of the second-floor windows of one of the warehouses. And I heard this voice. It wasn't vague or my imagination. It was real prominent, like it was fierce and strong, right in the center of my head.

"It shouted, 'ELWOOD!'

"I immediately slammed on the brakes and my head jerked around, turning to my right, in the direction of the voice. I remember looking back over my shoulder in the direction of the warehouse and factory windows. But there wasn't a soul in the entire area."

But, Bill added, within two or three seconds, he turned his head back to face front. Suddenly, out of nowhere, a huge 1930s touring car flew by, turning the corner at about 50 miles per hour.

He stared as it passed him, stopped and frozen in the street on his bike. He was only a few feet away from the deadly path of the large speeding machine.

"The car took the corner so fast it almost turned over," Bill recalled. "It was up on two wheels. It was back in the bootleggin' days. There were five or six or seven guys in there. And when it took the corner it sped off toward Market Street, like they were being chased.

"I think it was bootleggers or gangsters running from somebody. Maybe they had been in a rumble. It just busted out into the street.

"The timing was perfect. They would have hit me totally broadside, and I would have gone flying. My God! I woulda been killed. That's the truth. If that voice hadn't called my name— 'ELWOOD!' deep and demanding like—I swear I wouldn't be here talking to you today."

Shaken and terrified from the close call, Bill parked his bike and walked back, toward the direction of the voice. He hollered and looked in the first-floor doors for someone—anyone or anything—that might have called out to him. But the doors of the buildings were locked. The businesses were closed. There was no movement behind the dirty warehouse windows.

"There was not a living soul in that block," he said, shaking his head.

After admitting that he has thought often about his life-saving encounter with the unexplained, Bill said, "I've come to the conclusion, after 60-some years, that it was either what is referred to as a guardian angel . . . or Jesus Christ or maybe one of my deceased relatives. It was a man's voice, so maybe it was my father. He died when I was very young.

"I don't know who it was, but it happened personally to me. As a gentleman and as a fellow writer, I would swear to God, on my mother's grave, on my dead wife's grave.

"I'd have been mangled. They would have had to figure out who or what I was when they picked up the pieces. A person would be in a pretty bad way when he was hit like that."

Patty Cannon: Kidnapper, Murderess, Ghost?

I t's eerie at the small, three-way crossing where Reliance,
Maryland, meets Delaware. It's right on the North-South seg-
ment of the Mason Dixon line, a few miles west of Seaford,
Delaware, on Route 20.

Go there at night, if you dare. It's quiet, real quiet.

"Deadly quiet," folks say.

Passing cars rarely stop. The drivers are on their way to someplace else, someplace important. Reliance is just a pass through
spot.

"Hardly nobody heads there no more," say the locals.

But years ago they did . . . quite a few, and many of those who
thought they were just passing through stayed . . . forever . . . and
were never seen again.

When the moon is hidden behind thick clouds, especially in
the fall, and the wind blows across the open fields and rustles the
leaves in the roadside trees, you can almost hear the screams.

Some say they come from slaves and their children who were
sold for a price, or from the throats of traders and travelers who
were murdered in their sleep for gold, or from members of the
gang, who were butchered so they wouldn't share the horrifying
secrets.

Talk to certain people, and, in a whisper, they'll admit having
seen horrifying spirits, hovering the fields and floating along with
the thick gusts of wind. Others, in strict confidence, report hearing
the cries of children and grown men, from the spot that used to
be called Johnson's Crossroads—and from small, unnoticed
islands up and down the nearby Nanticoke River.

47

Spirits Between the Bays

Some even believe there are bodies still to be uncovered, in the fields near the crossroads, under tall pines on the islands in the river, and back in the black, dark woods outside Sussex County hamlets. Those in the know even speak of hearing rattling chains and seeing "with me own two eyes" old, pitted human bones— some lying exposed on the walkways of the secret underground tunnels that still exist behind hidden passageways under stately Victorian and Federal mansions from Georgetown to Snow Hill and Princess Anne.

But the modern sophisticated newcomers scoff at these "silly tales of the natives," offering such comments as:

What kind of backward, uneducated people believe in ghosts?

Undiscovered remains! Total, absolute nonsense!

Who ever really saw a restless spirit?

Secret passageways? . . . What delightful imaginations these quaint, country folk must have!

And why, in heaven's name, would these so-called "ghosts" choose to hover near Reliance, of all the out-of-the-way, no places on earth?

Patty Cannon is the answer.

In books, she has been described as Delmarva's most famous "murderess," a "woman of mystery" and "a bloodthirsty killer."

To her present day descendants, she is just as mysterious and fascinating.

George Figgs, now of Stewartstown, Pa., whose family tree is rooted on the Eastern Shore, grew up in areas known as Box Iron, Griddletree and Figgs Landing.

Relatives, especially his Aunt Midge, who is married to a Deal Island skipjacker, became very interested in genealogy in the mid 1970s. She told him about their family history, and he listened intently to all of her tales.

"Aunt Midge verified that the family was definitely related to Patty Cannon," said George.

Based on what he had heard, George described Great-Great-Great-Aunt Patty as a "big boned woman, very strong, who was dark complected with long black hair and evil eyes."

She was a slave runner who would ship her human cargo down the Chesapeake out of Figgs Landing. He heard tales that her ghost still roamed, from Seaford and Georgetown to the Cypress Swamp and down into the Pocomoke Forest.

48

"If we misbehaved," George said, "we were told her ghost would come and cut our hearts out and eat them, and also that while we were sleeping she would come and stare at you. It was a blunt Eastern Shore method of getting your attention. To us, she was a vampire, a werewolf, a devil, an actual monster—like Dracula, Countess Bathory, like Jack the Ripper."

According to George, Aunt Patty and her band would hole up in the Cypress Swamp camps. It's also been said that in her homes and inn she built secret passageways and tunnels, so she could get away from the authorities and pass undetected into river hideaways and the swamps.

George described himself as a Poe scholar, who has been obsessed since he was nine years old with the famous Baltimore poet. "I've always been deeply fascinated by the dark side and the paranormal," he admitted. "I guess it's part of my heritage."

If it's true that for every good there exists evil, and that each heart of gold is balanced by a horrifying creature capable of inflicting suffering, pain and death, then Patty Cannon most certainly was the dark balance in the simple, good-bad equation of life.

During the 19th century, the people on Maryland's lower Eastern Shore and in Delaware's counties of Sussex and Kent, associated Patty Cannon's name with fear, hate and dread.

Her story has been told many times, often with different details, some reaching intense heights of horror and gore. Scholars believe Patty's saga will never be told accurately. No one, including her family and gang, knew the real story of where she came from and who she was.

But a mixture of folklore, newspaper articles, eyewitness accounts and hand-me-down tales have given us a dark, shrouded portrait of the woman who has fascinated Delmarva residents and researchers in the 167 years since her death in 1829.

So, through a combination of research, legend, folklore and imagination, we offer a tale depicting the type of incidents that may have happened in Patty's inn at the crossroads of Reliance.

The two men, boys really—19-year-old Thomas, a bit taller and stronger built than his 17-year-old brother Martin—pulled their horses to a stop and raced toward the steps of the old house, standing at the three-way crossroads outside Seaford.

Spirits Between the Bays

It was dark, very late, a few minutes beyond midnight. Rain was pelting their clothing. They had pushed their horses through the narrow trails from the ferry, heading toward the inn that the boatman so eagerly recommended.

Little did they know that the bearded, one-eyed ferryman was in the employ of the innkeeper and received payment for each lodger he sent her way.

"Thanks to the kindness of the Good Lord, we made it," shouted Martin, stomping his feet to shake off as much rain and mud as possible.

Less enthusiastically, Thomas whispered, "From the looks of the outside, this is one step above a pigsty and will serve us only until first light. I also suggest we look at what we might be offered to eat and rely on our own provisions if necessary."

Rolling his eyes, Martin began to protest his older brother's concern. But his comments were never realized, for the innkeeper suddenly opened the door, and the two young men were distracted by the glow of flame from the lamp she held in her hand.

"Travelers! Welcome into my humble inn." Her voice was shrill, but lilting. The sound and cadence of a cunning spider, experienced at lulling its prey into a welcoming web of eternal rest.

The glow of the flame highlighted her dark hair, unkempt and streaked with gray. Dark red coloring accented her lips. A blue and white gingham dress was soiled with dark spots of dirt, perhaps blood from butchering.

The brothers had to look up to take in all of her massive, overwhelming appearance. Standing slightly more than 6 feet tall, she had the build of a livestock farmer and the breath of a load of rotting fish.

"Greetings, Mistress," said Thomas. "We were sent by the ferryman for overnight lodging. We'll be gone at first light."

"Folks call me Patty. You do the same," she said, leading them into the front room. A small dining table, set with plates and cloth for breakfast, seemed too neat and contrasted with her personal appearance.

She must have servants to do this work, Thomas thought, already wanting to ride on and take his chances overnight in a gully or makeshift lean-to.

"Where be ye bound, lads?" Patty asked, as she poured two glasses of dark red wine.

"Phila . . . " Martin started to answer.

But, almost shouting to drown out his brother's honest response, Thomas said, "North!"

"And your business, *up North*?" Patty asked, smiling at Martin and handing him a soiled metal goblet.

"We're meeting one of our father's merchant ships, to deliver the crew's wages," the younger man said. He did not see the dread in his brother's eyes, nor the effort that Patty made to keep a smile from escaping from her toothless mouth.

"Well, it's late," she said a bit too quickly, "and you'll need an early start." Leading them into a first-floor chamber with one single bed, she added, "It's all I have left, but there's extra bedding for the one who will be on the floor. You'll be able to hear us up and about, have food early and be on your way."

"Our horses," Thomas said.

"They've already been put into the barn. My people have done this before. We're accustomed to late evening arrivals, and we do all that's right to make your stay most pleasant."

Thomas and Martin smiled, still staring at the odd, mammoth figure as she closed their door.

Martin began to talk, but, putting his upraised finger to his lips, Thomas signaled silence. Together, with pantomime instructions, the brothers lifted a large bureau and placed it across the doorway, making it impossible for anyone to enter in the middle of the night.

Patty Cannon smiled at their actions, which she watched through a knotty pine peephole that provided her a view from the adjoining room.

She could see them whispering, then watched as Martin took the bed to sleep and Thomas sat on the floor, opposite the doorway. With a hunting knife in his hand, the older brother kept watch for an hour directly beneath the window.

Patty was patient. Experienced in the arts of ambush, robbery and death, she waited for Thomas' head to bob and, eventually, fall to his chest and not rise.

"He's asleep," she whispered to Diggs, her favorite lieutenant. "Kill them both, and I want the money, NOW!"

"Any preferences?" the bearded murderer asked.

"No," snapped Patty. "whatever suits you. Just keep it quiet and do it in haste. I don't want to arouse the other guests. They

51

never saw these two merchant boys come in. Besides, the others aren't worth killing, but these two are. I can sense a good jingle of coin from these two young ones. Such a shame they have to go early, but such is life . . . and, more so, death."

Diggs, one of Patty's most trusted killers, crept out the back door and around the side of the house. The window in the boys' room was closed with only two old shutters. It purposely had no lock and could be opened with a special handle attached to the outside.

Quietly, Diggs pulled on the window handle. The opening was wide, big for him and two other felons, Hobbs and Bernard, to climb inside.

Barefoot and bootless, the trio bounded into the room. Within seconds the deed was done. Hobbs shoved a razor-sharp knife into Thomas' chest. The older boy's eyes saw only a second of life before he died. He made no sound. No final breath escaped his lips.

As blood ran down Thomas' body, soaking the money belt and clothing, Diggs and Bernard pounced on the younger boy, strangling him in his sleep.

Two more murders at Johnson's Crossroads were over in less than one sweep of the second hand of a watch. Two more unsuspecting souls destined to wander the cornfields of Reliance.

Swiftly, the trio lifted the dresser from the doorway and waited for their mistress to enter.

With lamp in hand she stepped over the lifeless, strangled youngster and then bent down, reaching toward the brother wearing the blood-soaked money belt.

Breathing heavily, like a vulture hungry for dead meat, a vampire lusting for hot blood, Patty used a fraction of her strength to rip the wet strip of cloth off the body.

The trio of killers stood in the corner of the death chamber, waiting for her to offer some approval of their skillful work. As she looked inside, her breathing became heavier. Sitting on the floor, unconcerned that the fresh young blood was being soaked up by the back of her blue dress, her body became rigid.

Angrily, she snarled, "Who killed the boy?" her crimson-stained hand pointing at the body near the window.

All three had known fear, but none like the terror that engulfed the dimly lit room.

"M-m-mm Me. . . . I . . . ," stammered Hobbs, his body visibly trembling.

"Come here," Patty ordered, wiggling her finger to beckon him close to her. When he came within reach, she grabbed his hair and pushed his face against the dead boy's money belt. Hissing, she asked, "What is this, fool?"

"Mm-on-nnnee-y?" he guessed. With his eyes so close to the belt, he couldn't see anything clearly.

"Wrong, fool." The intensity of her anger allowed only a snarl to exit her throat. Her rancid breath only an inch from his cheek. "It's blood money, you fool. Half of it covered with red blood. Half of it useless and ruined and wasted. All because of your haste, your carelessness . . . your stupidity."

He stammered, tried to make excuses: *The boy moved*, Hobbs whispered. *The knife slipped . . . . I didn't know about the belt . . . .*

But Patty heard nothing. She saw his mouth moving. Saw the red stain of blood from the belt that she was pushing against his lips. Slowly, she brought Hobbs' face and the thick money belt together. Evenly, she raised the level of pressure until he was forced to stop talking. Hobbs gave a final, gurgling, crackling gasp, then stopped breathing. The room became silent.

But Patty didn't stop. She kept applying force, shoving the cloth money belt into Hobbs' mouth. Diggs and Bernard looked on, silently, in total fear, knowing their partner was already dead.

Then, as the lamp's flame began to dim, they heard the loud "SNAP!"

Hobbs' neck had broken. Diggs and Bernard shivered at the sound.

Patty, suddenly, released Hobbs' lifeless face. His head hit the floor, bouncing once. In the hushed room of death, the lifeless murderer and his still warm victim stared at each other, side by side, their souls sharing the fate of other unlucky victims whose bodies rested somewhere beneath a crop of dry, rotting Reliance corn.

Fearing for their lives, the remaining duo froze.

Patty, smiling walked to them, looked down, raised her hand and patted them both on the shoulder.

"Fear not, Diggs, and you, too, little friend. I've satisfied my anger for tonight. Let this be a warning to you both. Now, clean this up and dump them into The Room. Who can say what new good fortune we'll have tomorrow."

They nodded, forcing smiles as they began to follow her orders.

Suddenly, Patty stopped at the doorway, turned and smiled. "I feel good now. You can have the saddles from their two horses as payment."

They nodded, grateful for more than the saddles. Thankful she was calm and that they probably were going to see the dawn.

Then, she exploded in laughter, so loud and shrill that it most certainly should have awakened the guests. Their blood ran cold as she turned and approached them again. Diggs knew his life was over. Bernard began to make up a silent prayer.

Standing beside them, Patty smiled, told them to look into the money belt, and asked them what they saw.

"I . . . I . . . don't know. . . " said Diggs, his voice low, uncertain.

"Look again, fools. Now tell me or I'll snap your necks as sure and that dead idiot's over there."

Bernard leaned closer, sure he was to be dead within seconds. Summoning up his courage, he said, "It's good . . . . The boy's money . . . it is . . . it's good."

Patty slapped him on his back so hard that he fell forward to his knees. But he was smiling. Patty was laughing. That was a good sign, Bernard thought.

Diggs was relieved, smiling. He even forced a weak laugh.

"Right! It's good. The blood never touched the money. It's all good!"

"It's good," Diggs said, repeating it two, three times. "It's good! It's good!"

His wide eyes met Bernard's. He, too, was chanting, "It's good! It's good!"

The three exchanged smiles then turned and looked at Hobbs' lifeless, silent body, still staring at Thomas, who had finally stopped releasing his blood.

That's when Patty roared again. It was wild, crazy, demonic—a murderer's cry, a possessed, evil sound.

"This is my lucky day," she said, the words almost a witch's chant, proclaiming her glee. "One less share to give, one less mouth to feed, one less idiot to deal with."

Then she turned, stared at Diggs and Bernard, and snarled, "What are you two fools waiting for? I want them, all three of them, in The Room. Now!"

❖   ❖   ❖

Unfortunately, the stories of Patty Cannon are unfamiliar to many of Delmarva's younger residents, depriving them of one of the area's richest sources of legend and lore.

But older folks remember the stories of horrifying incidents that occurred mainly in Sussex County, Delaware, and in nearby Caroline and Dorchester counties in Maryland.

There is only space here to offer the highlights. But these, hopefully, will encourage some to visit the local library and read about the amazing life of Patty Cannon—Delmarva's most famous murderess and 19th-century serial killer.

In the early 1800s, Patty Cannon and her gang operated an inn west of Seaford in the border town of Reliance, Maryland.

Basically, she made her living, and fortune, by killing the travelers who came by to spend the night. She disposed of the evidence by burying bodies in her fields and garden and keeping the victims' belongings as spoils of her time and effort.

It's said she had The Room in the cellar, where she stacked many of the unburied corpses and kept them until, eventually, there was nothing left but irregular groupings of scattered bones.

Patty also made large sums of money by operating a sort of "reverse" Underground Railway. In the early 1800s, she and her gang stole free blacks from the northern counties and states and sold them to traders who took the unfortunate captives back down South.

From this, she made quite a good living.

Patty kept the slaves chained to the walls in her attic, above her bedroom, until the buyers arrived. She manacled others to trees on nearby islands in the Nanticoke, which was convenient for loading them onto boats bound for the Slave States.

There's a story in George Alfred Townsend's 19th-century novel, *The Entailed Hat*, about Patty's gang raiding a stately home in the center of Dover. Now known as Woodburn, the building is the state of Delaware's official Governor's Mansion and is open to tourists.

Townsend's chapter relates how Patty's gang was attempting to steal a group of slaves who were hidden in the building's basement, awaiting transport to safety in the North. According to legend, local authorities arrived to chase the gang from town, and one slavenapper, who was hiding in a tall tree that is still on the property, slipped and was strangled when his neck was caught between two branches.

Residents say the chains, still attached to the slavenapper's hands, rattle in the night and he is thought to be one of the four more prominent ghosts that still roam Woodburn.[1]

Eventually, Seaford area residents noticed that a fair number of people were going into Patty's inn, but few of these folks were coming out. Parents told their children when they were bad that Patty Cannon was coming over to get them.

This quieted them down quickly, since Patty was known to hate crying babies and despise children, especially when they caused the slightest fuss.

She is said to have beaten small children to death by crushing their skulls with blows from heavy tree limbs. One slave woman's child would not be quiet, so Patty stopped the child's cries by shoving the baby's face in the hot coals of the inn's fireplace until the child stopped breathing. Probably, these victims joined others in The Room.

Patty was not arrested or captured red-handed at the scene of a crime. Instead, she had left her inn, site of countless crimes and murders, to entertain rich ladies on the Eastern Shore with tales and stories. It's said her audience thought she had a wonderful imagination to think up such legends of suspense and horror.

Little did they know the real-life sources of Patty's local folktale repertoire.

Before leaving Reliance, the mistress of death rented her land to a local farmer. While plowing a field behind the inn, his horse fell into a hole and he discovered a trunk, containing what he thought was pirate's treasure.

Unfortunately for him, and more so for Patty, the chest offered up the dead body of a Georgia slave trader, wrapped in one of Patty's tablecloths—obviously another victim of Patty's unique brand of Southern Delaware hospitality.

The Georgian had come up to Reliance with $15,000 in gold to purchase slaves. Patty sat him down at her table and, while he was dining on her homemade vittles, stabbed him in the back, then tied up his body with her tablecloth and had her gang put him to rest right out back.

[1]See "Residents of Woodburn," in *Opening the Door,* 1995, Vol. II of the Spirits Between the Bays series, by Ed Okonowicz.

While she was living in Maryland, one of Patty's old gang members was captured for an unassociated crime. To help save himself, he agreed to testify against her.

With the traitor's help, an indictment against Patty and several of her gang was issued in April 1829, charging her with four murders It was believed that she was involved in up to 10 times that many.

Somehow, Patty was enticed to cross the state line and return to Delaware. When she was captured in May 1829 and the charges against her filed, news of the arrest spread quickly in towns and villages through Delaware and the Eastern Shore. Delmarva's most famous murderess was under lock and key in the Georgetown, Delaware, jail. Her trial was set for October.

Sometime in May, Patty disappointed those who were eagerly awaiting the gory tales she would tell in the Sussex County courtroom. She killed herself in her jail cell by taking poison that she kept in the hem of her skirt.

But Patty Cannon's story did not end with her death.

According to official records, she was buried in a pauper's grave behind the Georgetown jail, where her body rested until the end of the century.

At that time, Patty's corpse, and several others, were to be moved because an addition was being built to the original building.

According to a document—written by the late Alfred W. Joseph, dated May 2, 1963, and now on file in the Dover, Delaware, Public Library—in the early 1900s, James Marsh, a Sussex County deputy sheriff, was involved in the exhumation of Patty's casket for reburial in another potter's field.

"Somehow, while moving these bodies, Patty's skull came into the possession of James Marsh," the document states.

When Mr. Marsh moved to Colorado for health reasons in 1907, he gave the skull to a relative, Charles I. Joseph, for keeping. It was kept on a nail in the family barn until the late 1930s, " . . . by which time it had become quite a curiosity. To save it from damage or possible theft, he put it in a box and stored it in the attic of his home," according to Alfred Joseph's statement.

After his father's death in 1946, Mr. Alfred Joseph took possession of the skull and, in 1961, put it on loan to the Dover Library . . . where it sits to this day, in a round, red hatbox in the workroom on the first floor.

According to Bob Wetherall, Dover Library director since 1989, people occasionally call and ask to see Patty, and he agreeably responds to their requests.

Several national periodicals, including *Reader's Digest*, have called and inquired. Some have sent photographers to capture Patty's jawless, toothless remains.

Many who have seen the skull question whether it really is that of Patty Cannon. Some claim it's too small, since Patty was said to be a very large woman. But, the real answer will never be known.

"It's an interesting curiosity," Wetherall admitted. "There's no way of authenticating it. We usually bring her out at Halloween and tell ghost stories. And we've not had any sightings."

Author's note: An ornate metal historical marker, designating "Patty Cannon's House," stands at Johnson's Crossroads, at the Maryland-Delaware border at Reliance. The historic structure, now privately owned, is believed, at one time, to have been Patty Cannon's residence. Other research, however, indicates that the existing building was the inn and that the slavenapper's house has been torn down and actually was located several yards away.

Books on Patty Cannon:

Anonymous, *Narratives and Confessions of Lucretia P. Cannon*, 1841, New York, N.Y.

Giles, Ted—*Patty Cannon, Woman of Mystery*, 1965, The Easton Publishing Company, Easton, Md.

Shields, Jerry—*The Infamous Patty Cannon in History and Legend*, 1990, The Bibliotheca Literaria Press, Dover, Del.

Townsend, George Alfred, *The Entailed Hat*, 1884, Harper & Brothers, New York, N.Y.

Haunted Horses

Mention thoroughbred racing to Joe Average and he immediately thinks of "My Old Kentucky Home," racing at Churchill Downs and calendar scenes of stallions grazing behind white fences on thick Kentucky bluegrass.

Those in the business know better. Maryland is right up at the top when it comes to horses. The Free State is one of the best horse breeding regions in the world, being the home of a such racing legends as Kentucky Derby winners War Admiral (1937) and Northern Dancer (1964).

A large number of horse breeding and training farms are located in Cecil County, and most are clustered on scenic acreage just south of the Chesapeake & Delaware Canal.

To maintain operations, there is an small army of trainers, grooms, horse movers, veterinarians, jockeys and, of course, wealthy owners.

Randy was one of these horse people, and he loved his job.

To him, working outdoors was the ultimate high. Sure, his hands froze and ached in the winter, and summertime humidity was no treat. But the smell of dry leaves in the fall and springtime's soft breezes and rain made up for the uncomfortable seasons.

Very early in the morning, in the fall of 1988, the fog was thick, making visibility a flat out zero. Randy, then 24, pressed the limits of his memory, slowly trying to recall the route and winding turns as he guided his pickup through the back roads of southern Cecil County. The countryside he was carefully navigating is the largest of all the agricultural preservation areas on the Eastern Shore.

A horse handler, he was heading to work. On this particular day, he had been scheduled to arrive two hours earlier than his normal 6:30 a.m. start.

"I was all alone that morning. No one was up when I got into the barn area," Randy recalled. "It was unusual for anyone to be in that early, but I had to get some of the horses ready since we were shipping them out in the morning for a race out of state."

The fog had not thinned, and Randy walked through the heavy mist, reaching out with his hands to make sure he didn't walk into a barn wall.

"I had never seen anything like it. It was eerie, creepy. When I finally walked into the opening of the barn, I made my way to the time clock, which was located right in the middle of the building."

The barn was long, with the sliding doors open at both ends. Twenty-four stalls, each about 12 feet square, took up the interior. They were equally divided with a dozen on either side, each facing a duplicate box across the wide central aisle.

"It was a neat old building, built in the '40s," said Randy. "It was cold in the winter and the walls sweated in the summer. I remember standing all alone in the center of the barn and looking at the fog, it was crawling in at either end, rolling in from the outside, and heading toward me from both sides. It looked really cool, mystical, kind of eerie."

Randy said he checked his watch, which read 4:15 a.m. He had 15 minutes to kill before he was able to punch his card in the time clock.

"They didn't like us punching in early, so I just hung around, waiting. The barn was empty and quiet . . . dead quiet," he recalled. "I was the only one that had to be there that morning."

The building where Randy was standing was used only a few months of the year—usually during training in the summer—for one-year-old horses. It was known as the yearling barn, and it wasn't unusual that it would be empty, he said.

"I heard hoof beats on asphalt," Randy said. "It was at the end of the barn, past the fog line, to my right, coming in from the outside fields. So I figured it was somebody bringing in a horse for shipping out to the race, and I didn't really pay it any mind. But then, for a second, I thought: *That's funny. I thought I'm the only one that's supposed to be here this early.*"

Randy noticed that the hoof falls were getting closer, but they were softer than usual.

"The surface was asphalt, both in the center of the barn and nearby outside. When a horse's hooves hit the ground, it's usually hard and heavy, and makes solid thumps. When you've got 1,000 pounds hitting the ground all at one time on each leg, it makes a nice hard, real thick thud. It will leave an echo sometimes. Well, I'm starting to think it's a little odd, because it sounds like it's walking on tiptoes."

Turning, Randy squinted to see into the white-gray mist, to figure out who or what was coming.

Slowly and steadily, the dark outline of a man began to take shape. As the figure moved closer, Randy said, the person appeared to be about 70 years old, with gray hair and wearing a red-and-black checked shirt, denim jeans and thick, black work boots.

"He was walking towards me," said Randy, "totally silent, and he's leading this horse with a rope. It was a chestnut, red haired, a decent size, about 15-16 hands, and it had a white blaze across it's face.

"But the guy, he's kinda looking off into space, like he don't even notice I'm there. He walks down the center of the barn, right past where I'm standing. Now I'm looking at him real hard, but I don't recognize him. But to me that's not strange, because I'm fairly new. Only been working there about three months at that time."

As horse and handler got within six feet of him, Randy turned away to check the time clock and to look at the shipping paperwork. He heard the horse pass behind him. The hoof beats were slow, but still faint.

"I decide that I'll wait until he puts the horse in the stall and then talk to him," Randy recalled. "So, while I'm studying my papers, I hear the stable door bolt slide back, hear the horse go in the stall. I hear the door shut and the sharp sound of the latch being closed. So I figure: He's done! Then I turn around and start to walk to where they went and . . . . I swear . . . there was nobody in the aisleway of the barn.

"I walk toward the stall, and there's no horse in the stall. At that moment, I call out to the guy, to see if I can find him or get him to come back, 'Hey, Buddy! Where are ya?'

"I heard my voice echo in the empty barn. There was no sound. Nothing. No swishing of a horse's tail. No chomping on hay. No rustling of straw. I decided to check every stall, on both sides of the barn and at both ends, even the side they didn't go into. I tell you, I went to each and every stall and there was nothing. There was nobody."

Alone, with fog rolling along the floor, covering his feet, Randy stared and wondered.

"I'm thinking I'm going crazy. *Has my mind finally snapped?* It was so quiet in the barn, I could hear the time clock click on the quarter hour. It hit 4:30. I had been there for 15 minutes and it felt like it all happened in a few seconds. That snapped me back to reality, and I thought it was a ghost, straight up."

Randy left the barn immediately, going out the entrance away from where the phantom horse and handler had disappeared. He waited for a few of the other workers who were to arrive later, then returned with company to the scene of the spirits.

Being relatively new on the job, Randy didn't want to make waves or be labeled as odd, so he didn't tell anyone about the experience in the fog. About a month later, he met Andrea, another farmhand who had been assigned to the horses. One day, while they were on break, she shared a similar story that had occurred to her in the yearling barn.

"I hadn't been there that long," said Andrea, "when I had heard someone mention the Ghost Mare. We were talking about a problem with low water pressure and someone said, 'That's the Ghost Mare drinking all the water. That's what caused the pressure to go down.' "

Later, Andrea asked a few of the old-timers about "this Ghost Mare stuff," but they laughed if off as a horse farm legend and superstition. But a few people told her they had seen a horse in a stall, but when they looked again it was gone. Other times, someone would claim to have seen a horse walking down the aisle of a barn, but it would disappear.

"I thought that was kind of cool," Andrea said. "I had been around ghosts before, so to me it was okay. I've got an open mind about that stuff."

Andrea's job was to clean down the stalls—muck them out and replace the bedding and water for the horses—so things would be fresh when the horses came in from the fields. After the stalls were cleaned, Andrea would stay behind alone and use an electric blowing machine to clean up the final stray pieces of straw and litter from the barn's central aisle.

It was 10 o'clock in the morning, sunny and clear. The entire horse farm was alive with activity. Andrea was using the blower and glancing from side to side and behind, carefully making sure of where she was going.

"I caught a movement, and noticed a guy leading a horse through the barn," she said. "I immediately cut off the leaf blower and pulled the electric cord out of the socket, because I didn't want to spook the horse or make it have to walk over the cord.

"The guy was leading the horse on its left, away from me. He had a lead rope and was wearing blue jeans. It was a bay mare with a star on its forehead. I said, 'Hi!' and I got no answer. I thought to myself: *You rude so and so!* Then I watched them go by, heard them pass out of the barn and started to turn on my leaf blower."

Immediately, two other workers came into the barn and Andrea stopped to asked them the name of the groom who was leading the horse that had just walked through the barn.

Both of the workers said they saw nothing.

Disturbed by the incident and their responses, Andrea went to a friend who claimed to have seen the Ghost Mare.

When she described the horse's color, white star on the forehead and approximate age, her friend confirmed it was the Ghost Mare.

"My jaw dropped," said Andrea. "It was really very eerie. That guy just stared straight ahead, not saying a word. And the horse, she was so close to me, I could draw a picture of her. She was a beautiful horse. But what struck me as funny was that this was a yearling barn, and she was a few years old. So she shouldn't have been in there.

"She also walked very quietly, even though it was on asphalt. It was not the normal sound of a horse that size. It was kind of muffled. What really bothered me is that I was within six feet of them, and I spoke to the guy, who was about 25 or 30, and he didn't say 'Hi' back. After I realized what I might have seen, or probably saw, I got the chills.

"But I really wish I'd have gotten a better look at them," she said.

Randy agreed. "When I think back on it now," he said, "I wish I had experienced it more. I even wish it would happen to me again. I would try to walk up to him, or touch him, or pet the horse. How often do you have an experience like that?

"You always wish, your entire life, to see a ghost," he added. "But when you do you become scared and are taken aback by it. You don't react the right way at the time. You freeze and ask yourself: *Am I crazy? Am I seeing things? Did somebody slip something in my coffee? What is this I'm seeing?*"

Randy paused, as if he was considering his next statement carefully. "Your first instinct is to run and get away," he said. "Now I wish I'd have stayed around. I went back to that barn every day, as I clocked in. The first week after it happened I hoped I didn't see it. I was actually scared to go back in there. Then, later, I was almost looking for it every day for the entire year."

There are several opinions about what Randy and Andrea both experienced in the same place.

Randy suggested that it might be the roving spirit of an employee of the estate, maybe someone who was so comfortable with his surroundings that he doesn't want to move on.

"The wealthy people who own the farm had lifetime employees who were there forever," said Randy. "Maybe when this old worker died, he just stuck around 'cause that's all he knew. He was dedicated to the end, and when the end came, he just stuck around to make sure the horses were cared for properly. That's my opinion."

That might account for the handler, but what about the Ghost Mare and other restless, spirited horses?

According to several sources, horse graveyards are common on the training facilities and horse farms on the Eastern Shore, and elsewhere.

Carved gravestones and metal plaques bear the names of million-dollar money winners. In some farms, tall trees and landscaped shrubbery are used to mark the final resting places of famous racehorses and other less well-known, but equally loved, animals.

Burial ceremonies at horse cemeteries can cause the owners and workers to break down in tearful good byes.

"I've been there when they bury horses," said Randy. "I've assisted in putting them in the grave, and I've cried and shed some tears myself. You look around and even the roughest, toughest barn crew are brushing away tears from their eyes.

"To me, and others, it's hard when some of them have to be put down because of age or arthritis problems. Usually, the end is made as easy as possible. A lot of the horses are really loved. It's like putting down a dog or a cat, it's just bigger.

"The spot is selected, gravestones are put down after the ground settles. It all depends on what the owners want to do. On most of the farms, there's an area marked off as a special place for the animals they loved . . . a pet cemetery or horse graveyard. They call it by different names.

"But I love this job. The smell is terrible, the weather is harsh, but the horses . . . . Wow. When they look at you and they say thanks, you know it's all worth it. You see it in their eyes, or they'll put a head on your shoulder and give you a hug when they know you've helped them out. The horses talk to you in their own way. You look at a horse's eyes and you know what they're saying.

"But, I heard this saying once, and it's very true. 'If you work with livestock, you're going to work with deadstock.' It's just a fact of life."

Lady

The house of October Farm, located outside Easton, Maryland, dates back at least to the early 1800s. It's nothing fancy, just a standard two-story Colonial, Eastern Shore farmhouse that's shaped like the letter "T." The original brick is partially covered by yellow siding, all capped by a black roof.

My husband is a real estate appraiser and, at the time we first encountered our strange visitor, he researched the county deeds for a clue as to her identity. The earliest record available at the court house referred to a previous title that is nowhere to be found. But, many of the pre-19th-century records have been lost at the Talbot County Courthouse, so no one really knows when October Farm's house was actually built.

We do know that it originally was called Homewood, and that the house had been constructed in sections during different times throughout its history. The oldest part has a cellar, with a dirt floor and wooden pegs that keep the beams together, since nails were not available in those early years.

My husband's family owns the farm, and we moved into the house after we were married.

Our first child, Renee, would never sleep through the night until she was four years old. Once she was able to talk, she would tell us about a woman who visited her while she slept. I thought the story was the concoction of a four-year-old's vivid imagination, as well as an explanation of why she never wanted to go to bed.

Eventually, my husband and I joked about our daughter's mysterious and imaginary "Lady."

There were times, however, when I would wake in the middle of the night and every light in the house would be on. I'd get up from bed, turn them all off, only to awaken an hour later to find the lights lit once more.

In the morning, no one owned up to turning on the lights during the previous night.

My husband and I assumed our mischievous daughter had been up to some childish pranks, until one evening when Renee spent the night with a friend. Once again, the lights came on after midnight. I turned them all off, only to find they were lit again.

Finally, I walked throughout the house, turning off the lights and saying, "Okay now, Lady. That's enough! The lights have to stay off when we sleep."

That seemed to work, and I used the tactic on many subsequent occasions.

One of the incidents that I will never forget was when my mother spent the night because I was very ill with the flu.

The next morning, she said to me, "I saw you taking Renee to the bathroom last night. You should have let me take her. That's what I'm here for."

I was confused by her comment. I hadn't been awakened by Renee in months. The child finally was resting through the night and was not disturbing my husband or me.

Renee, then about five years old, was sitting at the kitchen table eating her cereal and listening to our conversation. She looked up at us and said, "Mommy didn't take me to the bathroom. The Lady did. She always does so Mommy can sleep."

I was startled by Renee's comment. I didn't know whether to be concerned about our paranormal house guest or laugh it off as the workings of an over active imagination.

Several years passed. We had two other children, both girls. There were times when toys would move across the floor of their own accord. There was a doll-sized baby carriage that seemed to be the Lady's favorite.

We joked comfortably about the Lady's presence whenever something unexplained occurred. The ghost was a constant companion to our family of five, and we didn't fear her in any way. She eventually became our guardian, a warm and comforting presence.

We soon would discover the extent of the interest and power of our protector.

The farm house was heated with kerosene oil heaters that were placed in the living room, kitchen and family room. Each was connected to a fireplace by a metal flue that sent the hot gases up the chimney.

Spirits Between the Bays

These stoves had electric fans that ran to keep the heater's metal casing from getting too hot as the high-temperature fire burned. The heavy blanket of heat kept the downstairs too warm and the upstairs barely above freezing, even on the coldest winter nights.

One particular evening was very windy. Torrential rain beat against the sides of the house with the intensity and sound of a hurricane. The temperature was just at freezing, and as the evening progressed past midnight the rain turned to ice.

We had tucked the children safely beneath their warm quilts, each in a separate room upstairs. My husband and I were asleep in our downstairs bedroom.

I was awakened by Renee, tugging on my arm. She was about 12 at the time, standing at my bedside in a semiconscious state.

Rubbing her sleep-filled eyes, she mumbled, "Mommy, the Lady said that there is a fire. You must get up."

My first though was to tell Renee to go back to sleep, that she was just having a nightmare. But as my drowsy mind cleared, I noticed the faint scent of smoke.

I grabbed my glasses from the nightstand and immediately focused on an eerie glow, coming from the living room across the hall.

Throwing back the covers, I ran to the doorway and saw the kerosene heater, blazing bright orange against the inky blackness of the living room.

The electricity had gone off, leaving the heater without the fan that kept it from overheating. A vase of artificial flowers that had sat atop the furnace casing had melted into a pool of liquid plastic.

The next few minutes were a blur.

I screamed for my husband.

With oven mitts we struggled to turn off the oil lines that fed the furnaces, and we propped the back and front doors wide open to get rid of the black smoke that was filling our lungs and hovering against the ceilings.

Several hours later, after the furnaces had cooled and the fires burned down, the danger was over and I tucked the children back into their beds.

It was almost morning as I descended the stairs and whispered aloud, *"Thank you, Lady, for watching over us."*

Years went by and trivial things happened to let us know that our Lady was still about.

Whenever she was near, there was the strongest scent of sweet flowers.

When Holly, our youngest daughter, was two years old, I was awakened in the early morning darkness by the scent of Lady in my bedroom.

I actually thought I heard her whispering, *"Holly needs you. Go to her."*

After the furnace incident, I didn't take her warning lightly.

I entered the nursery and peered at my daughter, sleeping on her junior bed. Holly's back was to me. She seemed to be resting peacefully. I turned to go back to bed.

"Touch her," the phantom voice urged.

Turning toward Holly's bed, I sat and placed a hand on my baby's cheek, thinking she might have a fever.

Her skin was cold. Ice cold.

Flipping on the nursery light, I turned the child toward me and her normally rosy complexion was bright blue.

I panicked.

Grabbing her up in my arms, I searched frantically for her pacifier amidst the bed sheets, thinking she might be choking on it.

Quickly finding the pacifier beside her pillow, I laid Holly's small body across my legs, opening her mouth to try and figure out why she wasn't breathing normally.

I screamed. As my husband rushed into the room, Holly's breathing was raspy, a thin whistle that indicated she was alive but in serious condition.

I administered CPR as my husband drove frantically to Easton Memorial Hospital.

The doctors determined that Holly had asthma.

If we hadn't gotten to her when we did, she probably would have suffocated in her sleep. Now under medication, she lives a normal live.

Thanks to our Lady, our treasured daughter is alive.

Eventually, my husband and I longed for a home of our own.

His parents gave us a building lot that sits at the end of the long lane leading from October Farm. Our new house was finished and we moved in during the fall of 1992.

Immediately after we vacated the old farm house, my in-laws began remodeling it for the new tenants who would be moving into the historic home.

Spirits Between the Bays

Many of the plaster walls were cracked and impossible to repair, so we decided to tear out the plaster and replace it with paneling.

The workmen were ripping out the wall of the nursery when they discovered another wall behind the one they had just torn down.

Yellowed wallpaper covered the hidden wall . . . and, in the center, hung a small, faded picture.

A picture of Lady.

My husband called me at work to tell me what they had found.

In his hand was a portrait, a 19th-century era photograph, of a woman with a soft smile. She was seated, as if posing, her hands folded. There was some handwriting in one corner, but it was impossible to decipher.

Although the image was old and faded, the image yellow against a brownish background, I was so excited. I just knew it was a picture of our guardian, and I was thrilled that we could take her picture with us to our new home.

After that discovery, we never felt her presence again.

The people who moved into October Farm's house haven't noticed anything either.

I suppose the Lady finally went to her eternal resting place. I don't really know her name or what happened to her or what caused her to linger behind after her death.

But I do know she was gentle, loving and kind. She adored my children and tended them as if they were her own.

Sometimes, when I look at the remnants of her faded image, I wonder who she was, when she lived.

Maybe, sometime long ago, she may have lost a child.

Perhaps she died young and was unable to raise her own children. I suppose we'll never know.

In any case, I'll always be grateful to her . . . and I'll always miss her.

But our family will never, ever forget our Lady.

—Debby J. Lyons

The Ghost Child

Visit the Jersey Shore and you'll often see people standing on the edge of the beach, gazing at the ever changing seascape of waves, sand and sky.

Whether you've lived near the ocean since birth or are a first-time visitor from the Midwest, strolling the open beach and appreciating the majestic beauty of an endless horizon of water is a natural, comforting, hypnotic act.

But, for just a moment, imagine what other unseen entities may exist nearby, also viewing the white-capped Atlantic during your peaceful moments of meditation.

Some believe that—from the tops of seemingly empty dunes and on lonely, vacant balconies of historic Victorian seaside mansions—immortal, invisible souls also enjoy the rhythmic sounds of the surf rolling across the silent sand.

Whether the spirits perished in the shipwrecks along the coast, during accidents on shore, in barroom brawls or from natural causes in the coastal towns, some restless souls maintain a comfortable existence at the shore year-round, in an eternal state of silence.

Avalon, New Jersey, is a picture book resort town. It attracts tourists from near and far, many returning year after year for the familiarity of its quiet setting and peaceful charm.

The "Big House" is what some people call the town's well-known landmark. An old Victorian mansion, it was distinctive with its ornate wrought iron balconies and a wrap-around porch. The massive structure dominates an entire block very close to the sea, offering its lodgers a marvelous view of the beach.

Built around the turn of the century, the mansion boasts two sets of stairs, impressive tall ceilings and large spacious rooms.

Today, its eight bedrooms—three are large open dormitory-style chambers—and three baths can accommodate nearly three dozen guests or renters during height of the summer season.

Beverly loves the beach. Born and raised in the mountains of Western Maryland, she was thrilled after her sophomore year of high school, when she was invited by her cousin Kim to spend part of the summer in the Big House.

Neither of the two girls knew anything about the mansion's resident ghost.

"When I first went to the house, I slept inside, on the third floor," Beverly, an education major at the University of Delaware, recalled.

"My first experience was about four years ago, and I can still remember it very clearly. I was awakened in the middle of the night and saw a girl in a white nightgown, in the corner of my room. She was a teenager, about my age at the time, and she was just standing there. I just looked and didn't do anything. I hadn't heard any stories about a ghost roaming the house, so I just went back to sleep and figured it as just a shadow . . . or a dream."

The next morning, Beverly described the young girl in her room to the other residents. The long-time renters suggested that it was their ghost. Apparently, said Beverly, there had been numerous sightings and everyone acted very calmly about her first ghostly encounter.

"After that, I started sleeping on the porch," she said, smiling.

Margaret, Beverly's aunt from Pennsylvania, has been spending summer vacations in the Big House since the early 1980s. A real estate agent, Margaret said she is "fascinated with all of the aspects of the supernatural and loves stories about ghosts. I think we would be pretty arrogant if we assumed that we're the only living creatures."

Although she has never seen the ghost girl of the Big House, Margaret shared some of the stories she had heard from other summer residents.

Apparently, living conditions in the Victorian beach home are quite flexible, and the renters must be comfortable with dormitory-style living arrangements. On hot summer nights, in particular, people find it uncomfortable and become restless. As a result, some move to different rooms on various floors to find a cooler place to sleep.

One night, after moving about the house, but not finding a better spot to rest, a woman from Philadelphia returned to her original room and found someone sleeping in her bed.

Assuming someone else also had been restless and had found her room agreeable, she found another spot to spend the rest of the night.

The next morning at breakfast, she began talking about the heat and her discomfort the night before. She then asked the other guests if they knew who it was that had been able to spend the night in her unbearable room.

But, apparently, no one else had been making the rounds or admitted to staying in that particular room during the previous evening.

Startled, the woman described the phantom sleeper as having dark hair and wearing a white nightgown. Several guests smiled. Over the years, they had heard similar versions of the same story from others who also claimed to have seen the ghost.

During another summer evening, soon after sundown, two couples were seated in the living room, sharing drinks and conversation and discussing their children.

Suddenly, they all stopped talking and looked at the ghostly girl who had walked down the stairs, through the living room, into the dining room and then disappeared.

After seeing the young girl in her room, and, later, hearing what sounded like pictures falling off the walls in the middle of the night, Beverly refused to sleep inside the building. She and Kim felt safer outside, and they spent the balance of their summer nights sleeping on the mansion's porch.

"Even though I was on the front porch," Beverly recalled, "I was still scared and I was bothered by loud, crashing sounds, that no one else heard in the darkness. But a lot of people who stay in the house had seen other strange things, so I didn't think that I was crazy."

During one August afternoon, an older woman stopped by the home. The summer tenants discovered that the visitor's mother had cooked for summer residents of the Big House years ago. As a child, the elderly woman said she had spent her summers at the shore.

Margaret said they eventually asked her about the ghost and the woman's reaction was, "Oh, yes! That would be Charlene. She met an untimely death."

Unfortunately, that was all the visitor would share. She didn't know, or perhaps wouldn't say, anything else. No one ever discovered any more information from her about the origins of the ghostly child of the Big House.

But both Beverly and her aunt heard other versions of the origin of the ghost girl.

According to local legend, in the early 1900s, a number of physically disabled and mentally retarded children from wealthy families lived in a large estate on the Main Line, west of Philadelphia. During the summers, the children were brought to the Big House in Avalon to vacation at the shore.

Another story says the children were cared for by nuns from a Philadelphia convent who brought them to Avalon during the summer.

One can only imagine the traumatic circumstances, or perhaps the untimely death, surrounding the origin of the child ghost. Did she drown while swimming in the sea? Was there an accident within the home?

Perhaps the answer, if there is one, will never be discovered.

But people have different reactions following paranormal experiences. After several summers in the Big House, Beverly has noticed that she is less afraid.

"It's not that you feel unsafe," she explained, "because everyone had described the ghost girl as a calm, loving person. But for someone 14 or 15, it just felt scary and kind of weird, but definitely not unsafe. A lot of people have seen her. Maybe what I saw wasn't the ghost, but it definitely was something I've never seen before.

"At first, right after I saw her, I told myself I'm never going back to that house. But after hearing even a small part of the story of why she might be there, it's sort of touching. I think that the girl liked it there. Then I begin to realize, Wow! Somebody also enjoys this place as much as I do, and she's willing to come back and stay for eternity.

"It's been more than four years since it happened, and I'd love to see her again," Beverly said. "It would be really cool, especially now that I have more knowledge of where she came from. But I'd really like to be able to ask her how she became a spirit, and find out what she wants from us. Who knows, maybe she'll be back and I can catch up with her next summer."

Fright Night on the Jersey Shore

T he envelope came in the mail, its contents no different than many of the others. The sender's name—Marty Phillips—was printed in the upper left corner along with his address, in Kennett Square, Pennsylvania.

A mark in the appropriate space indicated Marty wanted to be placed on our *Spirits Speaks* ghostletter mailing list. But he also checked the line: "I have an experience to share. Please call me."

We agreed to meet for an early morning breakfast at Friendly's Restaurant, east of Newark, Delaware. He was tall, with blond hair, and arrived with a much shorter girl who wore a white sorority baseball cap.

We all shook hands, quickly getting through the introductions as we settled into a booth. That taken care of, we covered the basics: Marty, 25, worked in Center City Philadelphia as a technician for a computer repair company. Gerri, 23, his girlfriend, was a graduate student studying psychology at the University of Delaware. They had been going together for three years.

Marty opened a pale manila folder, containing a hotel brochure and a pack of color photographs they had taken during their overnight stay, during Gerri's spring break in April.

Over the next two hours, the young couple shared a story very similar to the events that occurred in Stephen King's novel *The Shining*. Instead of the ice and snow of the mountains, Marty and Gerri experienced their fright night on the New Jersey Shore.

And, more importantly, their story was not make believe. They swear it actually happened.

❖   ❖   ❖

Spirits Between the Bays

It started in the middle of the week, in April 1995, when Marty, Gerri and another couple—Dan and Rita—were driving toward Ocean City, New Jersey. They planned to spend a few days of spring vacation at the beach. At night, they were going to drive north, to hit Atlantic City, win a million bucks in the casinos, and never go back to school or have to work another day in their lives.

While heading over the bridge that linked the island to the mainland, Marty noticed a tall, odd colored building with a strangely shaped roof.

"I remember it was on a Tuesday. I was at the wheel," Marty said. "I don't know why, but I happened to see the weird roof as we were coming onto the island. It was sort of roundish, with strange looking peaks and towers. There were lots of flags flying from the building, too."

"He started shouting," Gerri said, "like a little kid, 'I wanna stay at the place with the weird roof! I wanna go to the place with the weird roof!' He kept repeating it. It was really silly, almost embarrassing."

The three passengers told Marty he was crazy, that the fancy looking hotel would be too expensive. Besides, it was not worth spending their gambling money on something like that. They should look for a cheap place to crash and forget his stupid idea.

But Marty wouldn't listen and said that since he was driving he would have things his way. He followed the streets that lead to the tall, jagged roofline, heading for the old-fashioned hotel.

He drove into the circular entryway leading up to the door. As Marty stopped the car, they were greeted by a uniformed doorman, who opened the passenger's door and gave them a courteous nod. Marty and Dan went inside.

"At first the woman at the desk was trying to get rid of us," Marty said. "She thought we were just a few kids out for a joke. But when I said I'd pay for the night in cash, in advance, I got her attention. It was high, $270 for the four of us for the night. A fortune for us, but I figured: 'Why not? How often would I get to stay in a fancy joint like this?' I had some extra money and convinced Dan to go along with me and impress the girls."

Marty requested a room with a good view and was given #969, a corner, ocean-front mini-suite on the top floor.

"We thought the guys were crazy," said Gerri, "but when we saw the room we were impressed. Two large double beds. A full

bath, with marble walls and a vanity dressing area. The room had
old Victorian-style furniture and even a maple writing desk, plus a
color TV and AC. It was fantastic. We even told them it wasn't
such a bad idea after all."

Since night life, and even guests, in the hotel seemed to be
non-existent, the happy foursome decided to have dinner in
Atlantic City. Afterwards, they spent the rest of the evening playing the slots and trying their luck at some of the casino town's
blackjack tables.

It was well after midnight when they arrived back at their hotel.
A security guard, who sat in a chair beside the main elevator door,
got up, unlocked the front door and let the four young guests into
the hotel.

They went directly to their room and stayed up playing cards
until about 1:30 in the morning. That's when Rita announced that
she wanted to take a walk around the hotel. Since no one else had
the energy to go with her, the slim redhead left to explore the
building on her own.

About 20 minutes later, Rita was banging on the door. When
Marty opened it, she rushed into the room totally terrified.

"She was hysterical," said Gerri, "I mean, she was bawling and
shrieking. She ran into the bathroom and I thought she was going
to throw up. I couldn't understand much of what she said, but she
was on her knees, on the floor, shouting that she wanted me to go
back downstairs with her.

"I said I wasn't going out at that time of the morning, and she
started screaming all over again."

From the fragments that Rita was blurting out between hysterical sobs, Gerri was able to discover that her friend went downstairs and got off the elevator at the level above the first-floor
lobby. On that mezzanine floor, she walked down a pitch black
hallway that had a very tall ceiling.

When Rita reached a set of doors, she pushed them open and
looked into an empty, darkened ballroom. Suddenly, all of the
lights turned on and old-fashioned ragtime music started playing,
very loudly. Rita also noticed that it was freezing in there.

"Now, I will admit," said Gerri, "that Rita is a very dramatic
person, but this was strange, even for her. So I'm thinking that
there she is, downstairs in a huge hotel, in the dark and all by herself. She's just imagining this whole thing."

Rita said as she moved away from the ballroom, she went further into the darkness, down an empty, carpeted hallway where there was a series of end tables with lamps, spaced evenly apart. The tables were set against each of the ornate columns that rose toward the ceiling.

But, as Rita passed each column and table, she said the lamp came on. By the time she reached the opposite end of the hallway, she looked back and all of the lamps on the tables were lit, but no one had touched them. No one else was there.

According to Gerri, the whole story was ridiculous. "There must be a party down there, I thought. Then Rita was still begging for me to go downstairs with her. It was the only thing that she wanted. Well, neither of the two heroes—Marty or Dan—were volunteering to check it out. Marty was scared, and Dan was dead asleep.

"Rita and I got on the elevator, and I'm thinking that this is all because someone forgot to turn the lights off, and she's downstairs in the dark alone. But, when we got off the elevator, I noticed the difference in temperature was incredible. It was like walking out of your house in the winter. It was freezing."

Gerri logically figured that they turned off the heat to save energy. But as they walked down the dark hallway, the first lamp turned on as they passed, then the second, then the next, just as Rita had said.

Gerri could feel Rita was squeezing her fingernails in Gerri's arm. "Relax. They're probably just set with motion detectors," Gerri told her.

Eventually, they came upon a small entryway into a restaurant, the Terrace Room. The two women were standing on the top of a set of steps, near the hostess station, looking down on the empty, dark room. It was filled with several dozen white-clothed tables and an impressive grand piano in the center.

Suddenly across the far wall, at least 70 feet away, the lights came on. They were tiny, Christmas-type lights that had been intertwined through the lattice grillwork that was against the wall.

"That's when I was starting to worry," said Gerri, "because we were well out of range of any motion detector. I looked at Rita and she was just standing there, with a very blank, freaky stare on her face.

"As I tried to get Rita's attention, a cold breeze shot by us. It was like something ran by, and it was very cold. Then, within sec-

onds, music started playing in the Terrace Room. It wasn't ragtime. It was scratchy sounding, sort of like when you play old 45s.
It sounded as if the record was really worn down and in bad
shape.

"I just did an about face. I was halfway down the hallway, back
toward the elevator, when I turned and saw that Rita was still
standing, frozen, on the top stairs of the Terrace Room.

"I ran back, grabbed her by the hand and said, 'We're going
back upstairs!' And she kept repeating, like she was in a trance,
'You see what I mean? You see what I mean?' "

Because too many of the bizarre events in that short amount
of time didn't make sense, Gerri realized that she too was getting
spooked.

"Pulling Rita inside the elevator, I hit 9 and the doors started
to close. But then, before they shut all the way, almost touching
together, they opened up again. They did that five of six times, like
someone was trying to get in or stop us from leaving."

With Rita huddled on the floor and starting to scream in the
corner of the unmoving elevator, Gerri was close to losing it herself.

"That's when I really got frightened, because I couldn't get the
door closed. I just really wanted to get out of there. When they
finally shut, which seemed to take forever, I was just about hysterical. I was doing pretty good until the elevator went crazy on us."

When they arrived at Room 969, Marty let them in. He could
see both girls had been through a horrifying experience. After
hearing only a few of the incidents, he announced, "I'm not leaving this room!"

As soon as things
calmed down, Rita
shared more details
about her first solo trip
into the hotel's
unknown.

She said when she
came back upstairs
alone, she noticed an
open door in another
room on their floor.
After peeking inside, she
went into the room. It

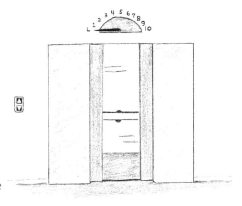

was as if she was drawn there, and it was very eerie, strange. But, she claimed she went through the room and came back out into the hallway much further down, as if she had been transported or magically floated through several walls.

Marty and Gerri listened, looked at each other silently and admitted they didn't know what to think.

At 2:30 in the morning, they awakened Dan. After quickly filling him in, they suddenly ordered him to remain still. Beside the glow of a low hotel room light, the quartet sat in silence, listening to eerie sounds creeping into their room from the hall.

"It was a kid crying," said Gerri. "I know that sound. I've worked with small kids in summer camp and I figured it was a little boy about four or five.

"It sounded like it was sobbing and lost, probably looking for its mother. Then, we heard a sound like it was walking down the hallway, dragging its hand against the wall, and passing right outside our doorway."

"I remember," added Marty, "that about that time, I looked and, I swear, I saw the doorknob to our room turn. It was like someone was trying to get in. Then, all of the sudden, it was like a strong breeze came under the door into the room. But it was freezing and the smell that came with it was horrible. I just never smelled anything like it."

"It was heavy," said Gerri, "a very potent or nasty kind of smell. We put our hands to our faces to try to stop from breathing it in, or smelling any more of it."

According to Marty and Gerri, the dragging sound against the wall and the twisting of the doorknob happened several more times, about a half-dozen times throughout that night. But no one in the room was interested in seeing what might be out in the hall or trying to get in their room.

They heard the little boy wandering for what seemed to be hours.

Also, the elevator across the hall kept going up and down. From about 2 to 6 o'clock, they heard the elevator doors open and shut, open and shut, over and over.

Sometimes, they thought they heard the sound of a mother calling out for the little boy, but they weren't sure. At one point, Rita, half asleep and still upset, announced that Burnaby was there, in the room with them.

No one knew what she meant, and, apparently, neither did she. Of course, with Gerri and Marty scared to death and Dan totally confused and frightened, Rita's tidbit about an invisible visitor did not have a soothing effect on the temporary overnight residents of Room 969.

Neither Marty nor Dan offered to open their hotel room door and look out in the hall. A few times, Marty said you could actually see the lock in the doorknob turn, as if someone had a key. When that happened he or Dan jumped up and twisted the lock so the door remained fastened from the inside.

"One time," Dan said, "I heard the rubbing against the wall outside the door, so I hit my fist against the wall a few times, to scare whatever it was away. Immediately, you could see our doorknob shaking, like somebody was out in the hall, trying to force it open and get in. That really shook us up."

At some point, Rita opened the door and tried to go out into the hall and look around, but Dan ran out, pulled her back in and slammed the door shut. Other than that, the four vacationers never left their room—except for Rita and Gerri's exploration around 2 a.m.

When daylight arrived, everyone was ready to leave early.

"I went downstairs," Marty said, "to pay for the long-distance calls we made, but the woman at the desk said there was no record of any calls from our room. That was crazy, because we all made a few."

Marty decided not to press the issue. It was just another strange event in the bizarre chain that had started hours earlier. It had been a long night and he wanted to leave, but he also wanted to see if he could come up with a few answers.

He knew from the hotel's classy appearance, fine brochures and expensive furniture and decor that it obviously catered to older patrons. He wasn't surprised that none of them were up and roaming around the lobby when he and his friends got in from A.C. at 1 in the morning. Even though the place wasn't full, he figured the occupancy rate had to be around 30 or 40 percent.

Starting to head back to his room, he stopped and turned. "The woman behind the desk was an older lady," Marty recalled, "and I looked at her for a minute, then said, 'You're going to think I'm nuts, and I'm not complaining or anything, but was there a party or some commotion in the hotel last night?'

"She looked at me very calmly and said, 'No. Why?' "

"That's when I told her about the people trying to get into our room, about Rita going into the freezing ballroom, and the horrible smell. The incidents were rolling out of me and I couldn't stop. She looked sort of surprised, but not really. You know what I mean? I expected her to laugh me off, but she just stared and patiently listened.

"I said, 'There was this woman calling for her kid, who seemed to be lost. She probably found her kid. I guess he's safe.'

"Without any expression, she looked straight at me and said, 'No, Sir. That's impossible. You see, you were the only four people in the hotel last night, except for the security guard.'

"That really got me. Then I asked if anybody ever complained about unexplained noises. I think she thought I was an idiot. She told me I had to talk to the security guard when he came back from an errand down the street."

Marty raced back upstairs to tell the others about the strange conversation. They all immediately finished packing and were ready to leave—as a group. No one wanted to exit the room and head into the hallway alone, or be left behind.

On the way out, they stopped to talk to the guard. The head of security came out, along with the hotel manager and the desk lady who had listened to Marty earlier.

They all stood in a group and listened to Marty, Dan, Gerri and Rita. One manager nodded quite a bit during the conversation. The security guard said he was there from 11 o'clock on, locked the front door and no one entered during the entire night except the four residents of Room 969.

To turn the lights on in the ballroom, Terrace Room and hall, someone has to access a circuit breaker box that is locked at 11 o'clock. And, the guard added, he did not hear the elevator move all night, and his chair was right next to the doors.

"But the thing is, they didn't think, or act like, we were fools," Gerri said. "None of them was shocked. They didn't say anything, like admitting it happened before. But I got the feeling that it did. I really thought they were going to blow us off, because we were just four young kids in a hotel, but they wrote everything down and took our names and phone numbers."

"Then," said Marty, "the manager asked us if we wanted to stay again—for free. It's a 300-buck-a-night hotel and she's offer-

ing us a free overnight. Well, after what happened, I had no inten-
tion of staying. I was packed and on my way out to the car."

"We asked about the name Burnaby," said Gerri, "and I don't
remember exactly what they said. But someone mentioned that
the owner had just died and that the place was being sold and
was going to be turned into condominiums."

According to Marty, the security guard was listening intently,
nodding and taking notes as Gerri talked.

"He was taking it all down, just like you are now, writing what
we're telling you. Nothing shocked him. He didn't blink twice. He
didn't try to explain it away, either. They didn't make any excuses.
They kind of nodded their heads and agreed with us. I really got
the feeling they had heard it before."

On the way home, the four adventurers agreed to keep the
story to themselves.

"We didn't want to tell anybody," said Gerri. "I know if I told
my mom she would ask me what kind of drugs I was on when I
was down there. We kept it quiet for a while, but then Dan told his
mother. Immediately, she told him to throw away everything he
had taken out of the hotel—ashtray, brochures, matches, sta-
tionery—anything he still might have from there. And he did. She
told him having the stuff would cause bad luck."

Thinking about it, Marty said there were other strange things
that happened: One of the rolls of film they used to take pictures
in the room disappeared; pictures didn't turn out from shots they
took with a different camera; and their hotel room door was ice
cold when the noises were coming from the hall.

"Most people would be packing their bags and getting out of
there," said Gerri, "and there we were, taking pictures of the room
and the door. We were crazy."

Marty said it's all so strange, and there were several factors
that would have dramatically affected what occurred, or possibly
even prevented them from experiencing anything at all.

If he hadn't seen the weird roof and hadn't demanded his way,
or had not been willing to spend a small fortune to stay overnight,
they would have stayed in a cheap sleep outside of town and had
a calm, uneventful evening.

If they arrived on a different day the hotel would have had
more customers.

Spirits Between the Bays

Marty said the desk lady told him a convention was coming in on Wednesday, and he and his friends noticed some of the visitors arriving as they left that morning.

"I don't know why everything happened in the hotel early that Wednesday morning," Marty said, "and I don't know why I directed us there. Was it a coincidence? Was there a reason? I don't have any answers. Maybe the guy who owned it and died was mad because they were selling the place. Or maybe sometime, years ago, a kid was lost or died there.

"I know I'll never find the answers, but I know what I saw, heard and smelled. All of us do, and nothing will ever change that. And I'll never forget that night and what happened."

Every time Marty, Gerri, Dan and Rita get together, someone mentions their fright night at the Jersey Shore.

"And," Gerri said, "we all remind Marty it was his fault because he wanted to stay under at the hotel with the weird looking roof."

Laughing, Marty said he can handle the abuse—especially since its been months since that strange evening—but, he added, "I tell you, after we left that morning, we had plenty to talk about in the car on the ride back home."

Author's note: This story almost went undiscovered. Marty admitted that the letter he sent me sat in the back seat of his car for two weeks before he finally placed it in the mail. He was planning to rip it up, but something stopped him and he tossed it in the mailbox figuring that he probably would never hear from me.

This pattern of events is not unusual. Some ghost victims are confused and concerned about telling their story. Others, who shared their plans about contacting or meeting with me, were convinced by relatives or friends to change their mind. It seems their well-intentioned associates told them that publication of their story would result in religious fundamentalists picketing their front yard, National Enquirer photographers sleeping at their doorstep and invitations arriving in their mailbox to join every witches' coven in a 100-mile radius.

Such is not the case. The only result is an interesting story that is enjoyed and appreciated by the rest of us.

Rose & Crown
Restaurant & Pub

H enry Hudson, while searching for a passage to the Far East in 1609, was one of the earliest explorers to report discovery of the Delaware Bay. A little over two decades later, in 1631, the Dutch established a whaling town on the coast of what is now the state of Delaware. They named it Zwaanendael—meaning "valley of the swans"—because of the numerous swans seen in the area.

That original attempt at settling the Lewes area was short-lived. The village was destroyed by Indians within months. The site was not resettled until 1659, and the name was changed to Lewes in 1682. Despite its interrupted past, today the busy tourist, fishing and sightseeing center is referred to as the "First Town in the First State."

Throughout its existence as a sentinel of the lower Delaware Bay, Lewes and its residents have played important roles in the country's history.

Its legend and lore are peppered with tales of fishing fleets, sailing ships and buried pirate treasure—Captain Kidd and Blackbeard the Pirate are known to have sailed its waters and visited its watering holes.

In 1813, during the War of 1812, the town was bombarded by the British. The Cannonball House on Front and Bank streets was struck by a British projectile during the attack.

Lewes also was home to many who made their living from the sea, particularly river pilots who guided ships up and down the Delaware River.

In such an historic and colorful setting, at the point where the Delaware Bay meets the Atlantic Ocean, one might expect to find a fair number of restless spirits, be they phantoms from the sea, ghosts of the Colonial homes or specters in Victorian mansions that now serve as museums and bed and breakfast inns.

On a weekend in November 1995, during an early evening rainstorm that was particularly fierce, my wife and I were driving through Lewes, looking for a place to dine.

We noticed people moving about in the dimly lit Rose & Crown Restaurant & Pub, located in the bottom of an old brick building on Second Street. Trying to avoid the wicked weather, we rushed in for a warm meal. While sitting in a booth and waiting to order, I scanned the surroundings.

An exposed red, brick wall rose at least two stories above my head. Five, large colorful flags hung from the wall. Antique furniture, including wooden church pews, accented the dining area. Naturally, the thought entered my mind: A *roaming spirit would feel right at home here. It has just the right atmosphere to host a ghost, or even two.*

As casually as one can, I mentioned to the person who had seated us that I was a sort of ghost hunter and writer. Then, before he had a chance to laugh in my face or abruptly turn away, I asked if the building had any ghosts.

I discovered that I was conferring with John Lester Jr., one of the pub's owners.

To my delight, very calmly and with no awkward reaction, he smiled and said, "Yes. I think so. But you should talk to Donna Jackson. She's been here for several years and has a number of interesting stories."

Six months later, I returned to the Rose & Crown. Seated in a secluded corner table, I spoke with Donna Jackson and John, her husband.

She had been a bartender at the restaurant for more than five years and knew the regular crowd very well.

"We have a good mix here," she said, "regulars who come in all year, from all walks of life. Then, there are the people who come back every year, for vacations. Some I don't know by name, but I recognize their faces, so I know I've seen them before."

John described the Rose & Crown as an "English-style pub, a comfortable gathering spot where everybody feels at home. It's a local place, open all year." Suddenly, offering a quick smile, he added, "Thank God, or we'd all starve."

Donna, who had made up a sheet of notes prior to my arrival, explained that we were seated in the glass room, also known as non-smoking room #2.

She said things seemed to start to happen in the spring of 1992, soon after the former owners tore out two old bathrooms that were located in that area of the building and created the dining room where we were talking.

"I used to say to them, 'It's funny. Maybe you disturbed something when you changed things around.' But they ignored me. They never experienced anything."

Donna's first unusual event occurred near the bar's main cash register. It would become the hot spot site of several unexplained incidents. While talking with another bartender, Donna said she felt something blow directly on her cheek.

"I immediately turned. No one was there. I must have turned pure white. The other bartender said, 'What's the matter? You look like you saw a ghost.' She later said all the color had drained from my face.

"I didn't know what to think. I'm very skeptical about things. I just put it out of my mind at the time."

About six months later, on Halloween night, a regular customer was standing near the cutout corner of the bar, close to the cash register, talking to Donna. While leaning on one leg, he felt something, like a single finger running up the back of his leg.

"He didn't say anything at the time," Donna said. "Later, when he told me about it, he said he turned around and there was nobody within 10 feet of him. He said he smiled and said to himself, 'Oh, well, I guess it's here with us tonight.' "

One day, just before lunch, around 11 o'clock, Donna was working behind the bar. Only one other person, a waitress, was in the dining room. Suddenly, Donna heard the sound of something rocking back and forth. It sounded like chair legs hitting the old wooden floor of the pub.

Looking up, she said, "I heard the rolling of feet, from side to side. I said to the waitress, 'Did you bump the stool when you walked by?' She said she hadn't moved for 10 minutes. She was standing still, playing the video machine.

"I told her to look at the tall barstool. It was still doing it, rocking, its feet lifting up off the ground, back and forth. She looked, saw it and turned away. It didn't seem to bother her, but I was amazed. It kept doing it for about a full minute, more than a dozen times, over and over. I can still hear the sound. Da-Dit . . . . Da-Dit . . . . Da-Dit . . . . I'll never forget that sound.

"I stared at it. I thought there definitely was something here. I'm the kind of person that says, 'Show me.' Well, after that I was a believer. Then, I thought of the poof on my cheek, the finger on the customer's leg. And I realized that all three things happened in the same area, near the small corner, cutout area of the bar by the cash register."

It was the following year, in the summer of 1993, when Donna had her most memorable and horrifying experience.

Alone about 2 in the morning, after closing, she locked up the restaurant, placed all the barstools off the floor and went into the small office to do paperwork.

"I heard the barstool start sliding across the ridges of the wooden floor," said Donna. "I've heard that sound thousands of times, every time people sit down or get up. I knew what it was. But then it hit me that all the stools were up on the bar. They weren't on the floor. Then it started.

"I heard Da-Dit . . . . Da-Dit . . . . Da-Dit . . . . It was the same rocking from before. I froze for a second, then got brave enough to peek around the corner of the room, looking out into the bar. That's when I got the chill. I shut the door and dialed Christian."

He was a regular who lived a few doors down the street, and he had told Donna if she ever needed help he would be over in minutes.

"When he answered the phone, I said, 'Christian. Do you believe in ghosts?' and he said, 'Yes, of course I do.' Then I said, 'Well, there's something in here with me. Can you come down?'"

At that point, with nervous terror mounting, Donna realized she had to leave the relative safety of the office to unlock the front door.

"I put the keys in my hand," she said. "My heart was beating a mile a minute. I didn't want to see what was out there. I flung the office door open, flew around the corner, and raced to unlock the front door. I just wanted to get out."

Thinking safety was within reach, Donna's shaking hand tried to place the thin key into the door lock, to allow Christian to enter.

But, as she looked up, the bearded face of a tall, thin figure was pressed against the outside of the frosted door glass. He was trying to see inside, and his fist was raised and ready to pound against the wooded frame.

"It was the scariest thing I ever saw," said Donna. "He's standing there, and I didn't expect him, and I jumped back, shaking all over. Thank God it turned out to be one of the regulars. He came in when he saw that I was totally fried. Then Christian arrived. I'm talking a mile a minute, frantic."

The two men stayed with Donna until she finished her work. Because she was so upset that night, Christian later said he waited a few days before he told her that he noticed a cold spot early that morning, as he walked back and forth from the bar to the kitchen area.

He pointed out the chilled area. It was near the first table on the left side of the aisle, just beyond the back edge of the bar.

One of the ghost's last visits occurred when John, Donna's husband, was seated at the bar . . . two seats away from the register, about 11:30 one spring morning.

"I'm half looking forward, toward the street and entrance," he said, "when I heard the sound of a chair dragging beside me. I thought it was somebody getting ready to sit down next to me, or one of the waitresses. So I called out, 'What do you want, Stacey?' But no one answered. I turned around and looked. The chair, it just moved, by itself. And all the time I thought Donna was sort of nuts. You know. Then, I said to myself, *Well, I guess there is a ghost.*"

Things have been quiet for about two years, said Donna. But that doesn't necessarily mean the spirit has moved on. Some of the regulars and older employees think it's still around.

Unlike other places that tend to give their resident spirit a clever name, the regulars and workers simply refer to their unseen guest as the Ghost of the Rose & Crown.

"I think they want to try to figure out who it is before they give it a name," Donna said. "But identified or not, I think there's something here. I don't think it wants to hurt us. It just wants to be noticed.

"But I will admit it scares the hell out of me sometimes, especially that night when I was here alone. I guess because I've had more experiences than most, I think it's trying to get my attention. I don't know why, but I do think it's great that it's here. I've always been fascinated with the unusual. I just never thought I'd have any first-hand experience."

According to Donna, visitors seem even more excited about a chance encounter with the pub's spirited presence.

"I've talked about it to a lot of people. The customers think it's great. They want to know all about it. People will come in and comment on how the place looks like an old English pub, and some will say, 'I've bet you've got a ton of stories. Any ghosts?'

"That's when I pause, look down and smile, then say, 'Funny you should ask.' I tell them I've had several experiences, and they hang on every word."

Historical notes: Buildings at the Rose & Crown's present location were destroyed by fire in 1932 that wiped out the entire block. The current structure, built in the 1930s, has housed a grocery and hardware store. A restaurant has been there since 1983.

Features: Open all year, seven days a week, the restaurant and pub caters to regulars, tourists and visitors. An ornate, original tin ceiling runs throughout the building. The Glass Room, a non-smoking dining area, features colorful stained glass and wooden panels from an English pub that dates to the 1700s. The Nook, immediately to the right inside the front door, is a popular dining site for small parties. The Stage, on a raised platform in the front of the restaurant overlooking Second Street, is often requested by couples.

Sightings: Table D-4, immediately past the end of the bar, and at the bar in the area near the cash register and video machine.

Contact: Rose & Crown Restaurant & Pub, 108 Second Street, Lewes, DE 19958; telephone (302) 645-2373.

Illustration courtesy of the Rose & Crown Restaurant & Pub

Dinner for Two

I t was our wedding anniversary. The ghost hunter and his won-
derfully charming bride. What would be more natural than to
celebrate the occasion with an intimate dinner for two at a
haunted inn?

Aiming to combine business with pleasure, I made a reservation for the last evening in November at "Settling Inn," a secluded
country restaurant, smack dab in the haunted heartland of the
Garden State.

"No problem," the voice on the phone replied, "we will seat
you beside the fireplace, at our special table for those who want a
memorable evening away from the other patrons."

I offered my thanks, and, before I could hang up, the voice
added, "We will even bring in Chef Otto to prepare your meal. He
doesn't work often, but is on call for such a special occasion."

I tried to protest, but was assured our anniversary evening
would be one we would never forget.

As we crossed the eastbound twin span of the Delaware
Memorial Bridge, I thought of all the major husbandly points I would
make, having pulled out all the stops for the annual celebration.

I had kept the details of the evening secret. As we drove east
on Route 40, my wife, Kathleen, thought I was taking her to one of
my favorite sites — the Atlantic City casinos.

I assured her our destination was out of the ordinary, and
would certainly meet with her approval.

I had read about Settling Inn a few years previously and
immediately placed it on my "must investigate" list of sites with
heavy haunting potential.

As we passed through a dozen small towns, fingers of the
famous Pine Barrens snaked across either side of the sparsely
traveled roadway. Turning north off Route 40, we drove through

the sandy landscape—following a rutted, winding gravel drive—until we arrived in a clearing. The parking lot was empty, but some lights were on and I could see some movement behind the candlelit windows.

Although it was obvious that the inn wasn't hosting a prom night dinner—and no senior citizen, bus tour crowd was grabbing snacks on their return from A.C.—the restaurant seemed to be open for business.

Thank God! I thought silently.

Since it was a week after Thanksgiving, the exterior was decorated for Christmas. Seasonal flags waved in the wind from the posts of the white wrap-around porch. Spotlights highlighted the gentle arches of green garland that were accented with bright red bows.

We parked near the steps that led toward the thick wood and ornate stained glass door.

As I helped her out of the car, Kathleen casually asked if we were at the right place. Before I could answer, a woman opened the door and announced, "We've been expecting you."

I smiled at my wife, who rolled her eyes, and I waved to acknowledge our receptive hostess. She was dressed in a full

length servant-style dress, more country than Victorian. Her dark hair was pulled back tightly, offering a painful appearance. Her heavy lipstick and eye shadow were highlighted by the bright beams shining onto the front porch.

The stern hostess held open the door as we entered the wide, candlelit vestibule. It took a few seconds for our eyes to adjust to the dim light of the yellow flamed candles that danced and flickered throughout. No electricity was apparent within the building.

"Welcome. Welcome, to our anniversary couple!" the hostess announced. The tone was stiff, like an emergency room nurse greeting her next patient.

After crossing our name off the reservation list, Miss Hostess grabbed two oversized menus and led us into a large dining room filled with over a dozen dark wooden tables sur-rounded by matching captain's chairs. All of the white lace table-cloths were accented with small vases containing miniature bou-quets of fresh flowers.

"Vivian will be your server," Miss Hostess announced, bowing slightly from the waist.

We looked over the list of selections, ordered drinks and made our choices known to Vivian, who appeared to be a younger version of our official greeter.

I went with the prime rib, Kathleen decided on the surf and turf.

As we chatted privately, four people seemed to take turns glancing in our direction: Miss Hostess gave us the eyeball each time she passed across the open doorway in the hall. Vivian stared as she traveled between the kitchen and bar. An unnamed workman, clad in a checked flannel shirt, glanced our way occa-sionally. And a white-hatted man, whom I assumed was Chef Otto, peeked out from the swinging kitchen door with the regularity of a wooden bird trapped in a cuckoo clock.

Almost 30 minutes had passed since our 6:30 p.m. arrival.

Proudly surveying my chosen setting, I commented that the Settling Inn's fire was warm, the atmosphere intimate and the ser-vice excellent.

"It should be," quipped Kathleen, "after all, we're the only ones here. In fact, there are twice as many people working here as there are customers—since it's only you and me as far as I can see."

"It's still early," I said, soothingly. "People around here proba-bly don't come out until later in the evening."

"Well, it's a good thing you made reservations," my wife added, her eyes laughing at her joke.

Vivian came to take away our salad plates and deliver the main course.

As she set the warmed dishes on the tablecloth, I noticed the workman, hostess and chef—lined up like three monkey's in a row—staring and smiling at us from across the room.

"Why are they watching us?" Kathleen asked Vivian.

"Oh," she turned and glanced at our standing audience, "they all know its your anniversary and want to make sure you're having a good time. We don't get many guests as happy as you two are, so they're sharing in your enjoyment."

Spirits Between the Bays

Kathleen rolled her eyes at me and asked, "What do you mean you don't get happy people. Who do you get here? I haven't seen anyone else in the place."

"I know, it's a slow night tonight, and it's still a little early," Vivian said, offering a forced smile as she walked away.

"Slow and too early, my eye," Kathleen whispered across the fresh flowers. "This place is weird. What do they do, cater to the late night vampire crowd on their way home after a feast of virgins at the beach? I tell you, you picked a winner this time."

"Relax, my dove," I said. "Try the food," I suggested, as I savored a perfectly cooked piece of darkened, moist beef. "Mine is delicious."

Kathleen tasted the lobster, then her steak, and agreed that the dinner was well prepared. She also mentioned that our viewing audience had disappeared.

"Probably getting ready for the rush of customers that's expected any moment now," she said, laughing.

We started talking about the past, the future. Like any couple at their anniversary dinner, we reminisced about the good times, which, on that night, seemed even better than they had been.

Bad times didn't exist, and the future would be brighter with unlimited potential.

We sat there, two people totally in love. The chemistry between us was exactly as it had been during our first night of passion and romance.

I held my wife's hand, squeezed it gently, and she responded.

I leaned forward, lifted her fingers to my lips and kissed her hand, softly.

A sound, a sigh, from the far corner of the room intruded upon our silent signals. We turned to see the backs of Miss Hostess and Mister Workman disappear around the corner.

The spell was broken, the aura shattered.

"I feel like we're being taped for *America's Funniest Home Videos*," Kathleen said. There was no trace of humor in her voice, only icy annoyance.

"Okay, so they're a little wacky. Maybe they don't see people like us much. We're special."

"Maybe they don't see anybody," said Kathleen. "I don't think anybody but unwitting strangers like us comes here. To tell you the truth, I have the feeling that this is the beginning of a nightmare, that it starts small and sweeps you up in a swirling, out-of-control spiral with the force of a tornado.'

"What are you talking about?" I said. "Look, this is no dream. The food is good, it's real. It's right there." I took another bite of my beef. "We both tasted it, right?"

Kathleen didn't respond. Her head was turned, her mind following her eyes as they surveyed the room looking for clues to the mystery she was creating.

"There's no electricity here," she said, still looking around. "The people are nutcakes. There are no other customers. Don't you find any of this a bit unusual?"

"No," I said, without hesitation.

Kathleen was quick with a response. "That's no surprise. After all, you spend your life talking to people who live with things that the rest of us can't see and who most other people think are a bit strange anyway. So . . . . "

"So what?"

"So, you wouldn't know strange if it came up and bit you on the side of your neck," she said. Then laughing, she added, "But that's a bad example, since some of your vampire friends do that all the time."

"Look, this place is perfectly normal."

"Sure, but normal in who's opinion? Yours and theirs," she said, pointing to the doorway where Miss Hostess had just passed and smiled.

"But," Kathleen added, "what if this place really isn't here? Maybe you and I are going to find out that this is one of those haunted places you're so crazy about finding, and that they want to get the ghost hunter inside and then drive him out of what's left of his previously normal mind."

Thinking a moment before answering, I weighed her comment. Then, like a flash out of the blue, the answer came like a bolt of lightning.

"You think this is a nightmare or a parallel dimension experience?" I asked, pulling out my wallet. "I'll prove to you this is real."

Looking around, I saw Vivian peeking from behind the doorway to the bar. I raised my hand and motioned for her to attend to our table.

Rushing to my side, she asked, "Is everything satisfactory?"

"Wonderful food," I said, "My compliments to Chef Otto. How did you like your feast, my dove?" I asked my wife.

Kathleen nodded and agreed, without much enthusiasm, that her meal was equally excellent.

We declined dessert and I gave her my credit card.

"Did you see that?" I asked, smiling proudly.

"What?" Kathleen inquired, a look of puzzlement covered her face like a mask.

"I gave her my credit card. When it comes back, I'll sign it, I'll take the receipt and we'll leave. Then, the receipt is the proof we were here. You don't get that out of a dream."

Kathleen didn't seem in a mood to banter and just smiled at my keen intelligence. "Well, you better leave her a big tip. It doesn't look like she's going to have a $100 night tonight."

Vivian returned. I offered my thanks for her attention and signed off on the receipt. As we rose to leave, she escorted us to the vestibule. Miss Hostess was there to hold open the front door, and Mr. Workman and Chef Otto waved from the kitchen.

"Nice, friendly group," I said, as I opened the car's passenger door for my wife.

"Yeah, friendly like a family of sharks. How would you like to have to spend the night stuck in a snowstorm with that crew. I'd shove the furniture against the door and stay up all night with a butcher knife in my hand."

The quartet had gathered on the porch, waving as I entered the car from my side.

I gave a final salute, started the car and backed up in their vacant lot.

"Try not to hit any of the incoming traffic on your way out," Kathleen said, sarcastically.

In my rear view mirror, I noticed that the inn's lights went out as soon as we hit the far edge of the parking lot and entered the gravel drive through the pines and brush.

When we were half way to the main road, still riding on the ribbon of rock, our car died—just conked out for no apparent reason.

Kathleen and I looked at each other. I shut off the radio and lights, then tried to restart the engine. It made no sound at all, only the lonely key clicking in the ignition in the dark.

"Well, you have any suggestions?" I asked.

"Maybe you can go back to the loony bin and ask your friends to use their phone," Kathleen said.

"You want to come with me?"

"My choices are sitting here, in the dark in the middle of nowhere, all alone, or going with you, right?"

"Right?" I said.

"Neither. I just want to wake up from this nightmare and find out I'm having breakfast at home."

"You stay here," I said. "Keep the doors locked. If there's a problem, honk the horn. Okay?"

"Okay," she said.

As I opened the door, she pulled me back into the car and whispered, "I don't remember when I had such an interesting anniversary. Can we do it again next year?"

I smiled, got out and shut the door tightly.

I had only taken 10 steps when the horn blasted. I raced back to the passenger door.

"What's wrong?" I shouted.

"Nothing," my wife smiled. "I just wanted to see if it worked and if you would come back."

I shook my head and returned to the gravel pathway. It took about five minutes to reach the far edge of the inn parking lot. But it took less than five seconds for my mind to register the most confusing and horrifying sight of the evening.

I turned and ran as fast as possible to the dead, darkened car, trapped in the middle of the woods.

Banging on the window, I shouted for Kathleen to unlock the door.

Jumping inside, I took the key and turned it fast and hard. Miraculously, it started.

"Thank you, God!" I shouted, as I floored the gas pedal and the tires shot bullets of gravel behind us into the air.

"Are you crazy? Slow down!" Kathleen screamed.

"Shut up and hold on!" I shouted.

In stone cold silence, I flew at 60 miles per hour through the rest of the narrow stone trail. When we hit the main drag, I pushed the speedometer over 90, heading west for home.

I wanted to put as much space as possible between us and Settling Inn. As we traveled west, across the middle of the Pine Barrens, I spoke in quick clips.

"I expected the lights to be off," I said. "I saw them dim when we were leaving. But I didn't imagine the rest."

"What? Tell me!" Kathleen shouted.

"It was gone. It was . . . I mean, it wasn't open. It was old and run down. Closed."

"What are you talking about?"

"I'm saying the whole damn building was falling apart, ready for the wrecking ball!"

I couldn't explain while driving, so I pulled off the side of the road, into a Wawa convenience store parking lot, careful to keep the car running.

I turned in the driver's seat, looked at my wife and made an effort to speak very slowly.

"I am telling you that the place where we just ate anniversary dinner was boarded up. There was no way we could have gotten into it.

"It looked like it was shut down years ago. There were no lights, no decorations, the porch roof was caved in. The place hadn't been painted in a hundred years. Every window was boarded up. There was no sign, no people. Nothing but a dump that's ready for the bulldozer."

"You're crazy."

I thought for a few moments before I answered. After all, it's not like I hadn't been accused of this before.

Calmly, and with conviction, I replied, "I'm not crazy. I'm just trying to tell you what I just saw."

"So we didn't have dinner?" Kathleen asked. "We didn't sit by the fire and see Mr. Woodsman and Vivian and chef, whatever his name is, with the big white hat?"

"I don't know about them. All I know is that, if they were, now they aren't. Couldn't have been. Not the way the place looks now."

"Give me your wallet," Kathleen said.

"Why?"

She wanted to see my credit card slip.

I pulled the worn, black leather folder out. She spread open the bill section where I always place my receipts.

It was there. Folded like it was when I shoved it inside, less than an hour before.

Under the Wawa lamplight, I unfolded the yellow paper, the dinner receipt that still bore my bold, carbonized signature at the bottom.

"I don't believe this," I said, passing the paper to my wife.

"It's blank," she said. "There's nothing on it except your name at the bottom."

"Weird," I said.

"Mega weird," she agreed.

"We've gotta go back," I said, starting to put the car into reverse.

"No way!" Kathleen said. "What are you going to do, wander around and knock on the boarded windows? Ask nobody who isn't there for the original copy of your receipt?"

"I don't know. I feel like we've got to do something. Okay, if we don't go back, then we better call the cops."

"Oh! That's really great. What are you going to tell them?" Kathleen asked, calmly.

I hesitated. "That we were just inside this inn, having dinner," I said, "and then, after our car stalled out, I went back to use the telephone, and it was closed up . . . like it had been shut up for years . . . ."

"Yeah," Kathleen said, "that sounds really good. Be sure to tell them about Mr. Woodsman . . . ."

"Workman," I corrected her.

"Oh, excuse me, we must get it correct. Mr. Workman and Miss Hostess and the other two ghosts."

I didn't reply.

"Then, when they ask you what you do for a living, be sure to tell them you're a famous ghost hunter and always take your wife out to dinner at haunted restaurants, to get more material for your next ghost book.

"They'll really like that. I bet they'll send out their best South Jersey version of Sherlock Holmes and Columbo to check out this hot case. Maybe they'll call *America's Most Wanted*, too.

"No wait! Look, over there—coming out of the Wawa with a deli sandwich and hot coffee—isn't that Robert Stack from *Unsolved Mysteries*?"

She was on a roll. I knew better than to interrupt, and, actually, I was sort of enjoying her monologue.

"But, now this is important, dear," she added, "don't take it personally when they all start rolling their eyes while you're talking. And I'd just agree when they *suggest* you take a breathalyzer test. Otherwise, they'll start fitting you up for a white, wrap-around jacket, the kind with all those floppy straps hanging from the sides."

"I guess it might be good to keep this to ourselves for a while," I agreed, considerably calmer by this time.

"Yes, dear. For a very, very long time," Kathleen said. "Let's just keep this little adventure to ourselves. Hopefully, when we wake up in the morning, we can go out to one of your favorite local gin mills, like Tomaine Tommy's, for a nice quiet liquid lunch. I know the atmosphere won't be the same, but, as my mother told me many years ago, a girl can't have everything."

I pulled out of the Wawa lot.

The rest of the anniversary drive home was very quiet and, by comparison, quite uneventful.

Author's note: Each month we carefully check our credit card statement to see if the bill will appear for our anniversary dinner at the Settling Inn. At the time of the publication of this book, no entry for that intimate November evening has appeared.

On each of our periodic trips to Atlantic City, I'm tempted to pull off onto the inn's nearly overgrown gravel driveway. But, a thick, rusted chain and battered "No Trespassing" sign bars the way.

Maybe that's just as well.

About the Author

Ed Okonowicz, a Delaware native and freelance writer, is employed as an editor and writer at the University of Delaware, where he earned a bachelor's degree in music education and a master's degree in communication.

Also a professional storyteller, Ed is a member of the National Storytelling Association. He presents programs at country inns, retirement homes, schools, libraries, public events, private gatherings, Elderhostels and theaters in the mid-Atlantic region.

He specializes in local legends and folklore of the Delaware and Chesapeake Bays, as well as topics related to the Eastern Shore of Maryland. He also writes and tells city stories, many based on his youth growing up in his family's beer garden—Adolph's Cafe—in the Browntown section of Wilmington, Delaware.

In 1996, he was host of *Ghost Talk*, a weekly television program that aired on Delaware's Suburban Cablevision. Ed presents beginning storytelling courses and writing workshops based on his book *How to Conduct an Interview and Write an Original Story*.

About the Artist

Kathleen Burgoon Okonowicz, a watercolor artist and illustrator, is originally from Greenbelt, Maryland. She studied art in high school and college, and began focusing on realism and detail more recently under Geraldine McKeown. She enjoys taking things of the past and preserving them in her paintings.

Her first full-color, limited-edition print, *Special Places*, was released in January 1995. The painting features a stately stairway near the Brandywine River in Wilmington, Delaware.

A graduate of Salisbury State University, Kathleen earned her master's degree in professional writing from Towson State University. She is currently a marketing specialist at the International Reading Association in Newark, Delaware.

The couple resides in Fair Hill, Maryland.

Pulling Back the Curtain

Volume
I

The first book in a series of true ghost stories. Relive 8 real-life ghostly experiences and enjoy 2 local legends.

"A treat from professional storyteller Okonowicz."
Invisible Ink
ghost catalog

$8.95

64 pages   5 1/2 x 8 1/2 inches   softcover   ISBN 0-9643244-0-7

Opening the Door

Volume
II

13 more true-life Delmarva ghost tales and one peninsula legend are sure to keep you up at night.

" 'Scary' Ed Okonowicz . . . the master of written fear—at least on the Delmarva Peninsula . . . has done it again."
Wilmington News Journal

$8.95

96 pages   5 1/2 x 8 1/2 inches   softcover   ISBN 0-9643244-3-1

Welcome Inn

Volume
III

Features true stories of unusual events in haunted inns, restaurants, and museums and "Concert by Candlelight," winner of a 1996 Storytelling World Honor Award.

". . . a sort of auto-club guide to ghosts, spirits and the unexplainable . . . ."
Theresa Humphrey, Associated Press

$8.95

96 pages   5 1/2 x 8 1/2 inches   softcover   ISBN 0-9643244-4-X